T0330336

INSURANCE
FROM UNDERWRITING TO DERIVATIVES

INSURANCE

FROM UNDERWRITING TO DERIVATIVES

Asset Liability Management in Insurance Companies

Eric Briys and François de Varenne

JOHN WILEY & SONS, LTD

Chichester • New York • Weinheim • Brisbane • Singapore • Toronto

Copyright © 2001   John Wiley & Sons Ltd,
The Atrium, Southern Gate, Chichester,
West Sussex PO19 8SQ, England

Telephone (+44) 1243 779777

Email (for orders and customer service enquiries): cs-books@wiley.co.uk
Visit our Home Page on www.wileyeurope.com or www.wiley.com

Reprinted October 2005

This publication is designed to provide accurate and authoritative information in regard to the subject
matter covered. It is sold on the understanding that the Publisher is not engaged in rendering professional
services. If professional advice or other expert assistance is required, the services of a competent
professional should be sought.

Eric Briys and François de Varenne have asserted their right under the Copyright, Designs and Patents
Act 1988 to be identified as the authors of this work

Other Wiley Editorial Offices

John Wiley & Sons Inc., 111 River Street, Hoboken, NJ 07030, USA

Jossey-Bass, 989 Market Street, San Francisco, CA 94103-1741, USA

Wiley-VCH Verlag GmbH, Boschstr. 12, D-69469 Weinheim, Germany

John Wiley & Sons Australia Ltd, 33 Park Road, Milton, Queensland 4064, Australia

John Wiley & Sons (Asia) Pte Ltd, 2 Clementi Loop #02-01, Jin Xing Distripark, Singapore 129809

John Wiley & Sons Canada Ltd, 22 Worcester Road, Etobicoke, Ontario, Canada M9W 1L1

British Library Cataloguing in Publication Data

A catalogue record for this book is available from the British Library

ISBN 10: 0-471-49227-2 (H/B)
ISBN 13: 978-0-471-49227-6 (H/B)

Editied, designed and Typeset in 11pt Palatino by Nick Battley, London, England
(http://www.nickbattley.com)
Printed and bound by CPI Antony Rowe, Eastbourne

Contents

Preface

"In 1980 the life insurance industry was 150 years old.
In 1990… [it] was ten years old."[1]

This statement by Gary Schulte, senior vice president of Executive Life, illustrates the dramatic change that has affected the insurance landscape. Indeed, not too long ago, life insurance was solely associated with protecting one's family against the dire consequences of early death, while nowadays life insurance companies tend to define themselves more as asset gatherers and managers. Henri de Castries, the newly-designated CEO of AXA, goes as far as saying that AXA's mandate is to provide its clients with *"financial protection"*. Increasingly, life insurance companies sell investment-orientated products, such as unit-linked policies, annuities in which the insurance element can seem rather remote. As a matter of fact, Richard M. Todd and Neil Wallace (1992) go as far as to ask whether Single Premium Deferred Annuities (SPDAs, as sold in the United States) can still be classed as insurance. Indeed, they claim that an SPDA, which is a policy which includes an option to buy an annuity at the end of the saving period, has much more in common with a financial instrument than an insurance policy. They justify their claim by noting that the annuity option is more like an option against unforeseen declines in long-term interest rates.

The same trend is also affecting the Property and Casualty (P/C) insurance industry. Admittedly, the pace at which the P/C insurance industry is "reinventing" itself is slower than that of the life insurance industry. Still, it is fashionable these days to talk about ART (Alternative Risk Transfer) and securitization of Mother Nature's hazards.[2] ART is an interesting area of business for P/C insurers, as it may bring some underwriting diversification benefits. For instance, insurance companies now provide residual value protection on sea containers or coverage against the coupon deferral and/or extension risk carried by some financial securities (such as the Tier 1 bank capital securities).[3] These risks

---

[1] *Quoted by Richard M. Todd and Neil Wallace in "SPDAs and GICs: Like Money in the Bank", Federal Reserve Bank of Minneapolis Quarterly Review, Vol. 16, No. 3 (Summer 1992).*

[2] *See, for instance, Morton Lane's website www.lanefinancial.com and the references therein.*

are new for insurance companies. They tend to fit nicely with other more traditional underwriting risk exposures, such as household, fire, theft, pollution, etc. On another front, AGF, the French subsidiary of Allianz Group, has securitized its Monaco earthquake exposure[4] by issuing earthquake-linked securities. In that particular case, the risk flow is the other way round. It is clear, then, that insurance companies bring new risks to the capital markets.

These transitions have not been smooth, though. Many American, British and Japanese policyholders, not to mention Lloyd's Names, painfully remember the bumpy episodes they have endured. Compared to the mutual fund business, life insurance is still a very opaque business. While the portfolio composition of mutual funds is very transparent, and the funds are marked-to-market on a regular and frequent basis, the portfolio composition of the general account of a life insurance company is far less transparent. Interestingly enough, Fred Carr, the controversial CEO of Executive Life, viewed policyholders as "docile lenders who would not ask questions".[5] It is fair to say that many American and European CEOs of life insurance companies have been, until recently, wholeheartedly sharing this view. Indeed, this is the proposition on which the growth of worldwide insurance players has been often predicated. In some cases, it worked — in others, it did not. It is also fair to say that the guarantees provided to policyholders by some governments acted as an implicit subsidy system for asset misallocation. Policyholders were reassured (if they worried at all) that they would benefit from the governmental safety net if their insurance company ended up in dire straits.

This book is about the insurance industry, both life and P/C. Its main message is that the insurance industry should be looked at from an "option" or "derivatives" viewpoint. It will be seen that insurance underwriting is tantamount to option writing. Such an analogy is not merely semantic—it entails far-reaching consequences, which this book

---

[3] *Tier 1 securities are debt securities that qualify for bank regulatory capital purposes. Indeed, they "walk and talk" like common equity: the bank issuing Tier 1 capital has the option not to pay the coupons due (provided certain objective criteria are met) and to convert it into a perpetual security.*

[4] *Nothing comes for free! The beautiful French Riviera is on a fault line.*

[5] *Quoted by Todd and Wallace in "SPDAs and GICs: Like Money in the Bank", Federal Reserve Bank of Minneapolis Quarterly Review, Vol. 16, No. 3 (Summer 1992).*

explores. The first two chapters are devoted to the P/C insurance industry, with the former concentrating on pricing issues, and the latter providing an overview of securitization of insurance risks. The third chapter takes a historical perspective and draws the lessons from the life insurance crisis in the USA during the "Roaring Eighties". The fourth chapter looks at numbers. More specifically, it examines European insurance companies' stock prices from an empirical standpoint, and "tortures them until they confess". The fifth chapter takes a normative view and explains how a sound Asset-Liability Management (ALM) framework can be put together within an insurance company. Again, an option angle is taken. The sixth chapter builds upon the previous chapters and shows how to interpret the increasingly blurred boundaries between banks, insurance companies and capital markets. The last chapter reminds the reader of the challenging issues brought up by the regulatory authorities. Last, but not least, an ALM survival toolkit has been provided in the Appendix. As investment bankers, and Microsoft® PowerPoint™ addicts, we know the value of concise messages, and we have designed the toolkit with this value very much in mind. Hopefully, this has resulted in a useful, and efficient, resource. In any event, we hope that we can convince the reader that the "option angle" is a unique and rewarding way of deciphering the insurance industry and predicting its future course.

If writing a book is the best way to run into intellectual debt, then a foreword is usually the best way to settle it! For us, this is our opportunity to thank our former students and also our many colleagues, both from the academic world (on both sides of the Atlantic) and from the investment banking community at Lehman Brothers, Merrill Lynch and Deutsche Bank, and not forgetting, of course, our clients. They have all helped us shape and sharpen our understanding of the fascinating world of insurance. A book also requires a publishing company and an editor. In that respect, David Wilson (now at TEXERE), Sally Smith, Benjamin Earl and Nick Battley have our gratitude for making a promise come true.

Last but not least, we would like to dedicate this book to our families. When we promise that this book really is the last, they act as if they believe us! Capucine, Flora, Clement, this may not be the last, but you can be sure that your dads owe you a lot!

Eric Briys and François de Varenne   *London, April 2001*

Chapter 1

The Basics of Property-Casualty Insurance

1.1 Introduction

According to the UK magazine, *The Economist* (16 January 1999), the non-life insurance industry (otherwise known as the *property-casualty* (P/C) or *property-liability* insurance industry) is in trouble. Indeed, *The Economist* argues that several signals point to an industry which is actually in dire straits. Specifically, the magazine highlights four main issues: the first, and perhaps foremost, is that insurance premiums are falling. Secondly, interest rates have plummeted. Thirdly, growth prospects have remained stubbornly gloomy, despite the rise in value of insured risks. Lastly, and almost adding insult to injury, the industry is said to be suffering from excess capital. For experienced insurers, none of these complaints appear particularly novel. For example, as *Standard & Poor's Europe Insurance Market Profile 2000* notes, underwriting losses (i.e. the excess of claims and expenses over premiums) have been soaring almost everywhere—in France, Belgium, Germany, the United States and Tunisia, to name but a few. In a nutshell, all the indications point to an industry which has somehow managed to transform itself into a loss-making concern. However, to clarify this suggestion, we need to start by revisiting the basics[1] of insurance pricing.

When analysing the earnings generated by their firms' diverse activities, property-casualty insurers tend to slice the pie into two readily-distinguishable pieces. On the one hand, there is the so-called

---

[1] *Basics does not, however, mean simple! Insurance pricing is indeed a subtle topic.*

technical result (or underwriting income) which represents the balance between products sold (principally insurance premiums) and expenses directly associated with insurance *per se* (principally claims and administrative expenses). On the other hand, the aptly-named *financial result* represents the income generated by the investment of the collected insurance premiums. Importantly, the time lag between the collection of insurance premiums and the payment of claims gives rise to investment opportunities.

Given this distinction between the two forms of potential income, property-casualty insurers tend to deduce an implicit business corollary, which they view as a reasonable economic basis for their activities. A good number of them believe, therefore, that a financially viable insurance firm requires not only that overall profits be positive enough to allow for a fair risk-adjusted return on invested capital, but also, by implication, that both segments (the underwriting and the financial result), should be seperately profitable on a stand-alone basis.

It just so happens, however, that in property-casualty insurance, this type of financial orthodoxy frequently fails to stand up to scrutiny. Indeed, underwriting generally produces deficits—which worry insurers and prompt them to hike insurance premiums. Furthermore, this is far from being a new phenomenon, as Figure 1-1, which is drawn from a study of the French P/C insurance market published by Briys and Husson (1987), clearly shows.

Figure 1-1 reveals that underwriting results in the French property-casualty business were invariably in the red from 1970 through 1984. Indeed, from 1974 through 1982, the underwriting deficit deteriorated by a factor of 6.2. During this same period, the total amount of premiums collected actually rose almost threefold! Briys and Husson take the study forward in a different light when, in the last column, they examine the ratio between *technical results* and *technical reserves*. Technical reserves measure the pending liabilities to the various policyholders and usually comprise the so-called *loss reserves* and the *premium reserves*. A company's loss reserve, computed by actuaries, is the amount set aside to provide for outstanding claims, both reported and not reported (known by the acronym IBNR, i.e. *Incurred But Not Reported*). As such, it is the insurance company's primary source of long-term debt. However, it is patently clear that this form of debt is far riskier than traditional debt. Indeed, neither the magnitude, nor the timing of its cashflows, is known in advance. Furthermore, claims

Year	Global result	Underwriting result	Financial result	Financial result / Global result	Technical reserves	U/writing result / Technical reserves
1970	441	−1,228	1,669	3.8	34,206	3.6%
1971	248	−1,588	1,836	7.4	39,648	4.0%
1972	673	−1,782	2,455	3.6	45,376	3.9%
1973	880	−1,492	2,372	2.7	51,911	2.9%
1974	846	−2,251	3,097	3.7	58,952	3.8%
1975	772	−3,087	3,859	5.0	66,853	4.6%
1976	666	−3,436	4,102	6.2	76,000	4.5%
1977	955	−3,887	4,842	5.1	85,308	4.6%
1978	1,462	−4,932	6,394	4.4	96,492	5.1%
1979	1,244	−6,376	7,620	6.1	109,940	5.8%
1980	1,401	−8,513	9,914	7.1	126,359	6.7%
1981	670	−11,134	11,804	17.6	145,123	7.7%
1982	1,159	−13,863	15,022	13.0	170,176	8.1%
1983	4,163	−13,729	17,892	4.3	194,001	7.1%
1984	4,789	−14,673	19,462	4.1	219,196	6.7%

Figure 1-1   Results of the French property/casualty industry

Source: Annual Report to the French president from the minister of finance

payments are often affected by extraneous factors, such as judicial decisions. The premium reserve, otherwise called the *unearned premium reserve*, corresponds to the balance of risks that are still to run after the balance sheet date. As such, it can be viewed as a form of short-term loan; indeed, most P/C insurance policies are written for one year. It follows, therefore, that the underwriting result over the technical reserves ratio provides, albeit imperfectly, an implicit interest cost of these technical reserves.[2] In fact, it was almost fifteen years ago that Briys and Husson argued that borrowing money from policyholders via the issuance of

[2] *This quantity is also called "the cost of float" by the legendary Omaha guru, Warren Buffet, as will be explained later in this chapter.*

insurance policies could be a rather costly exercise. These days, the real argument is whether this implicit interest rate is actually out of control.

Are we obliged, then, to echo numerous insurance professionals when they voice alarm about a situation in which a given level of competition seems to yield inexorably deficit-prone technical results? This question is important insofar as a true answer necessitates an in-depth examination of the price-setting logic often cited by property-casualty insurers. Indeed, we are compelled to ponder the actual foundation of the commonly-accepted distinction between results based upon technical activity and those stemming from financial activity. In other words, this apparent distinction begs the question as to whether, when calculating the premium, we should take into account all, or part, of the income derived from financial investments.

In this chapter, there is no intention to provide an all-inclusive model providing for the determination of insurance premiums. The goal is rather more modest. We present current thinking with regard to casualty-liability insurance rate-making and, in so doing, show that there are lessons to be learned and that these may be somewhat controversial.

In the first part of this chapter we scrutinize the propositions put forward by property-casualty professionals. We examine their usual ways and means of price-setting and focus upon the extent to which they manifestly fail to pass muster. The second part comprises a historical overview of the manifold pricing recommendations formulated at one time or another in the United States. Contemporary controversies on this subject are but the latest pages of a seemingly never-ending tale, of which the laborious opening lines cannot fail to remind the observer of the present-day debate between insurers and the insured. In the third part, we present the conclusions, which are supported by modern financial theory, with regard to the determination of premiums in a particularly competitive insurance market framework. In the fourth part, we examine potential obstacles to the application of these conclusions. The fifth part looks at how modern option pricing theory can be used to refine our understanding of insurance pricing. Finally, subsequent to a brief summary of the arguments developed, the conclusion touches upon some complementary lines of research and focuses more precisely upon fine-tuning the recommended model to transform it into a workable price-setting tool.

1.2   How the premium has traditionally been envisioned

The features specific to the functioning of property-casualty insurance firms have been subject to such a wide range of commentary that there is no need to cover old ground. Nevertheless, it may serve as a timely reminder to policyholders reading this that, in insurance transactions, the sales price (i.e. the premium) is collected before stipulated services, namely claims payments, are duly provided. Moreover, for a number of technical, medical and legal reasons, it is often the case that any claims settlement by the insurer may be spread over several years. Reference has often been made to an *"inversion of the operating cycle"* (Fourastié, 1946). Two basic corollaries are usually drawn: a) insurance pricing is a rather delicate actuarial exercise; and thus b) technical reserves must be built up to represent the liabilities towards policyholders to ensure that the inherent promises to them do not become failed promises. These reserves are then invested on financial markets and placed under the supervision of the relevant regulatory authority. This is precisely why insurance firms are usually viewed as fulfilling an important financial intermediary function (Husson, 1984).

Upon closer scrutiny, however, the activities performed by property-casualty insurance firms are not actually unique, despite first appearances. Indeed, all things taken into account, when real estate developers or motion picture producers, for example, sell or auction off accommodation or movies at fixed prices prior to their respective building or filming, they are also saddled with the same problem pertaining to cost price. On the other hand, food retailers, for example, accumulate cash before they pay their suppliers and thus have opportunities to invest such proceeds in the interim.

That said, it is nevertheless true that property-liability firms are constantly subject to both these situations. In the final analysis, though, any claims of originality made about the activities of property-casualty insurance firms is actually less significant than the opportunities for ambiguity that these peculiar characteristics seem to bestow upon countless insurance industry denizens. For example, in its comment on the Italian insurance market, Standard & Poor's observes that *". . . in the low inflation, low interest rate world of Euroland, underwriting losses at this level appear unsustainable even when investment income is taken into account"* (2000, op. cit.).

Consider the following: while emphasizing his primary role as a safety salesman, if not a security guarantor, an insurer principally considers the extent of the potential risks incurred. This overriding consideration forms the basis of most leading actuarial manuals; in them, we are urged to base insurance premium calculations upon the characteristics of claims probability distribution (see Bühlmann, 1970 and Gerber, 1975). This premium is formally elaborated as:

$$P = E(S) + k + R \qquad (1)$$

$E(S)$ represents the mathematical expectation of claims, k denotes ongoing company running costs, while R is a risk premium which allows for coverage of unforeseen deviations in the claims amount to be paid, but still provides the company with "normal" profits. In other words, this standard pricing mechanism relies upon the so-called "law of large numbers". Within a large, diversified and homogeneous underwriting portfolio, the claims burden should converge towards its expected value. However, we all know that the expected value is not, actually, to be expected. Hence, the actuary has to incorporate some safety loading on top of the expected value. According to the actuaries, such rate-setting logic thus applied is likely to yield underwriting profits.

Let us suppose, however, that this is not the case. The deficits incurred on the underwriting front are written off, notwithstanding the existence of the financial revenues obtained through investment of the technical reserves. In fact, equation (1) is construed in such a way as to ignore, totally and utterly, any and all additional income derived from the company's financial activities. Actuarial price-setting endorses the separation of the underwriting side from the financial side. We may also note that the premium designated as R (most often a function of the parameters of the claims distribution) is the result of an unassociated calculation. To put it differently, rates are established independently of any notion of market-based equilibrium, simply because the rules on which they are theoretically based are solely determined by supply-side factors (i.e. underwriting).

Yet an insurer may just as well focus on his activities as a financial intermediary. Thus he could promote his importance to the financing of the economy through his investments made on the financial markets.

However, this will in turn prompt concerns over his technical deficits: how is it that the vagaries of the financial markets can jeopardize this secondary activity—which matters so vitally to the nation, both from a social and economic standpoint (see Valin, 1984)?

It should go without saying that we have deliberately caricatured the arguments put forward by insurers; in reality, their powers of reasoning and self-justification are usually far more subtle and varied according to the intrinsic nature and the financial situation of the firms concerned.

Whether intentional or not, this reasoning—based as it is on the differentiation of the insurer's dual activities—stems from the very outset on a falsification of the debate surrounding property-liability insurance rate-making. Furthermore, it undoubtedly hinders the ability to make the best decisions with regard to both the portfolio management of insured risks and investment policy (see Briys, 1985). Of course, it should be noted that the controversy surrounding the setting of appropriate rates for property-liability premiums is not confined to Europe. It is striking to note that, in the United States, for example, this question of pricing is often the source of highly-technical debate, involving not only members of the insurance profession itself, but also the relevant regulatory authorities.

1.3 How price-setting recommendations have evolved in the United States

An initial attempt to get to the core of rate-making in the United States of America can be dated back to 1919. At the request of the Arkansas Insurance Commission, the National Convention of Insurance Commissioners (NCIC, 1919) was instructed to scrutinize certain features of fire insurance price-setting and, more specifically, to provide a satisfactory answer to the following question:

> "Whether any items of profit or loss connected with the so-called 'banking end' of the business could be properly taken into consideration (in the regulation of fire insurance rates)."

The posing of this question triggered the vehement opposition of American insurers (see Webb, 1982). Indeed, such was the strength of their protest that, despite the counter-arguments put forward by the Arkansas commissioner, the Convention produced a report in 1921 which concluded that rate-making should be purely technical and should not take into account a company's financial activities, whatever their size and scope. In the US, this recommendation goes by the name of the *"1921 Standard Profit Formula"* (NCIC, 1922). In specific terms, the Report laid down the rule that the technical profits of a fire insurance company should be set at 5% of the premiums collected, plus a further 3% of the same premiums for the purpose of covering and offsetting any potential catastrophic risks. Unfortunately, the report failed to offer any rationale behind the specific figures of 5% and 3%. Indeed, the sole explanation provided seemed rather curious, to say the least:

> *"An equitable regard for the investors who furnish the capital for this particularly hazardous business would indicate that 5% is the minimum percentage which can be regarded as a 'reasonable underwriting profit'. This has already been recognized as equitable by several states."*

Despite the fact that it had no theoretical basis whatsoever, this formula was nevertheless readily accepted and applied to virtually all property-liability cases until 1946. It was only in 1947 that the price-setting issue once again came to the fore, when the New York insurance managers addressed a new report—the *McCullough Report*—which had been made to the NCIC (which, by then, had been transformed into the NAIC). In this highly-detailed document, one paragraph bears special mention:

> *"The 1921 formula is in error in that it disregards certain investment income having its origin in the underwriting activities of the companies. The amount of this error is large and under present circumstances amounts to about 2½% to 3% of earned premiums. Investment income is inextricably woven with the underwriting activities of the companies. Apparently, this was recognized by the 1921 Fire Insurance Committee which saw fit to deal with the situation by allowing exclusion of all investment income in return for a reduction in the conflagration allowance from 5% of earned premiums to 3%. In relating investment income to underwriting profit, consideration of capital gains and losses should be excluded."*

Despite this, the Report was rejected by the profession, which saw to it that the 1921 formula remained applicable.

It wasn't until the end of the 1960s that price-setting aroused renewed controversy. The best-known episodes comprise the *Arthur D. Little Report* (1967), the *New Jersey Remand Case* (1972) and the *Massachusetts Automobile Rate Hearings* (1975). This last document is surely the most original of the three, since it contains the following declaration put forward by the Insurance Commissioner of the State of Massachusetts:

> *"It is absolutely incomprehensible to me how the industry could have successfully argued for so long that an underwriting profit margin should be programmed into the rates without regard for the investment implications of the business. It does not take an economist to know that if someone takes a dollar from you and returns $.95 one year later, his profit on the transaction was the sum of the five cents directly taken and the gain from the use of your money for the year's period."*

The debate provoked by this document involved numerous experts and proved highly contentious. In fact, it marked a major turning point: for the first time ever, the authorities agreed to dissociate themselves from the 1921 formula and, at long last, a new ruling recognized the senselessness of *ex nihilo* price establishment. It was thanks to the evolution of financial theory that the principle of market-based prices actually integrating financial income was finally adopted. According to a 1981 opinion poll commissioned by the *Louisiana Insurance Rating Commission*, some three-quarters of the American States either demanded, or at least advocated, pricing protocols similar to those recommended by the State of Massachusetts.

The new pricing recommendations are based upon the *Capital Asset Pricing Model* (known as CAPM) which stems from the efforts of Sharpe (1964), Lintner (1965) and Mossin (1966). According to Kahane (1979), the relevancy of this model to insurance-related conundrums is attributable to its capacity to address itself successfully to the three fundamental questions already mentioned earlier in this chapter:

- Should we, or should we not, take financial income into account when pricing and, if so, how?
- What means of measuring risk incurred should be incorporated into the calculation of the insurance premium? More specifically, should we content ourselves with the risk premium R currently proposed by actuaries?

- Is insurance pricing derived from the model compatible with the existence of a financial market open to competition, in which participants benefit from opportunities to lend and borrow on a level playing-field?

These three questions centre upon a common issue—the capital market—which has, until now, been studiously avoided by insurance professionals. The following intuitive example should allow us to shed much needed light upon this paramount feature.

We shall compare two firms that are starting up. One is a holding company and the other an insurance company. Their one common feature is that they invest 100% of their resources—debt as well as equity—in financial assets. That said, their respective forms of indebtedness differ markedly. In the case of the holding company, it is represented by bonds issued on the market while, in the case of the insurance company, it corresponds to technical reserves. For the purposes of this example, assume that shareholder outlay, leverage ratio and the composition of asset holdings are rigorously identical for each firm. Their respective stockholders consequently incur the same degree of risk. If the insurance market is perfectly competitive, these two groups should likewise draw similar profits from their outlays. However, it so happens that this is not the case when the insurance company records systematically positive technical results, as this situation simply translates into a negative cost of indebtedness! As a result, the insurance company assumes a positive rent. If the insurance market is competitive, new businesses will make their entry and so this phenomenon will continue until decreased premium rates completely absorb the initial rent. More precisely, the point of equilibrium is reached when the underwriting deficit of the insurance company is such that the cost of its indebtedness is identical to that which is borne by the holding company.

1.4 The pricing model of the State of Massachusetts

Given, amongst other things, the need to protect the rights of the insured, it should come as no surprise that the insurance sector worldwide is subject to rigorous auditing by regulatory authorities. One particular challenge for the latter lies in devising a system of pricing recommendations that simultaneously allows a company shareholder to obtain a fair return for his capital and avoids creating a form of economic rent which would be detrimental to the interests of the insurance consumer. One solution lies in the application of a model which, while assuming that competitive access to indebtedness is identical for all users, nevertheless precludes any and all anomalous rent from the very outset. The insurance pricing tool proposed by Fairley (1979) largely reflects, to this day, the actions of the Massachusetts Insurance Authority.

To a great extent, Fairley's approach is based upon the CAPM. In accordance with this model, the expected (required) return on a stock is equal to the risk-free rate, plus a risk premium—the level of which is proportional to the sensitivity of such stock to overall market movements (as measured by the beta coefficient). Put more simply, the required return on a given stock is equal to the price of time (risk-free rate) plus the price of risk associated with the stock. This risk is one that cannot be diluted away, even after including the stock in a widely-diversified portfolio. Indeed, this systematic risk merely reflects the fact that the stock "breathes" at the rhythm of the overall economy, which is itself usually reflected by an equity index such as the S&P500 or the CAC40. Of course, such stock may breathe at a faster or lower pace than the overall economy and it may, indeed, be more or less risky than the overall economy. In this framework, the expected return on an insurance company's equity (r_k) and the expected return on its portfolio of invested assets (r_a) are expressed as:

$$r_k = r_f + \beta_k (r_m - r_f) \tag{2}$$

$$r_a = r_f + \beta_a (r_m - r_f) \tag{3}$$

in which r_f represents the risk-free return, r_m the expected return on the so-called market portfolio (a proxy for the overall economy), β_k and β_a the respective beta coefficients (sensitivity coefficient to the overall economy) of the insurance company's equity (K), and asset portfolio (A). The total risk premium is thus equal to the product of the sensitivity coefficient and the risk premium carried by the market portfolio (i.e. the overall economy). Hence, the riskier the asset under consideration, the higher its expected return.

The insurance company's expected return on equity is also equal to the sum of the expected underwriting and financial results, divided by its equity (otherwise called its surplus), namely:[3]

$$r_k = \frac{mP + r_a(K + T)}{K} \tag{4}$$

in which m represents the expected underwriting margin, P the amount of underwritten premium, K and T the equity value and technical reserves, respectively. One can define two useful quantities: The first is usually known as the *funds-generating coefficient*. It is equal to the ratio of the technical reserves over underwritten premiums T/P. Of course, premiums do not give rise to immediate claims payments. In some insurance lines, such as liability, the delay can be quite significant while in others, such as car damage, claims can usually be settled in a much shorter time. The second quantity is known as the *premium-to-surplus* ratio, namely P/K. This is also an important quantity, since it provides an indication of the degree of insurance leverage taken by the insurance company. Since issuing insurance policies is tantamount to borrowing money to leverage asset investments, some insurance market observers readily compare insurance companies with hedge funds.[4] Hence, the expected return on the insurance company's surplus can be rewritten as:

$$r_k = ms + r_a(gs + 1) \tag{5}$$

---

[3] *For the sake of simplicity, it is assumed that the insurance company has not issued debt —either senior or subordinated. This question would make sense if taxes and/or regulatory capital issues were considered.*

[4] *This comparison may seem bold and it contains an element of truth. However, it would be more precise to talk about a double hedge fund (or a reverse hedge fund). Indeed, a P/C insurance company is leveraged as most hedge funds, but its leverage is already a bet in itself. The bet is doubled in the sense that some P/C insurance companies are tempted to invest in securities that are themselves significant bets (not to mention the "gambling for resurrection" strategy). For more on this, see Eric Briys and François de Varenne (2000).*

where s stands for the premium-to-surplus ratio and g for the funds-generating coefficient. This expression has a fairly straightforward interpretation—it simply begs the question: How does a P/C insurer make money? It states that shareholders' rate of return is achieved by leveraging both the underwriting return (i.e. the technical side) and the rate of return on invested assets (i.e. the financial side). The underwriting leverage is generated by the premium-to-surplus ratio. Indeed, the more the insurance company underwrites insurance policies, i.e. the more it borrows money from its policyholders for a given level of surplus, the more it leverages its underlying insurance business. The investment leverage is produced by both the premium-to-surplus ratio and the funds-generating coefficient. This makes a great deal of sense since, in its investment role, the insurance company is akin to a mutual fund that would source its investable funds via its own equity and borrowed money (see Cummins and Lamm-Tennant, 1994). Other things being equal, the higher the funds-generating coefficient, i.e. the longer the average time between the insurance policy inception and the claims payment date, the fatter the investment income flowing to the insurance company.

This straightforward return on shareholders' equity expression has a number of managerial implications and it lies at the core of the work of equity analysts covering the insurance sector for investment banks. For instance, in May 1997, Salomon Brothers' Global Equity Research Department issued a report entitled *Global Insurance: Creating Shareholder Value in a Consolidating Industry*. One of the main focuses of the study was an attempt to disentangle the various factors that are instrumental to a P/C insurance company's success:

> *"However, it is not necessary for an insurer to generate a profit from its underwriting in order to earn a return greater than a conventional investment company since underwriting also generates funds for investment upon which shareholders will reap the rewards. To the extent that these funds are generated at a cost lower than could be financed through money markets, so the underwriting activity should enable an insurer to earn higher returns on its own equity than could be derived through a conventional investment company."*

The same type of story[5] is to be found in a February 2000 Deutsche Bank report entitled *European Insurers: The Aviary*:

---

[5] *Remember, equity analysts love to tell stories, especially "success stories"!*

> *"The profitability of an insurance company is dependent on the following considerations:*
> - *the level of underwriting profit or loss, reflecting the pricing level of risk and the level of claims;*
> - *the level of investment yield, reflecting yields available in the market;*
> - *the level of investment pool relative to the underwriting return."*

Our expression (5) can also be rewritten along the lines suggested by the famous "Sage of Omaha", Warren Buffet, who happens not only to be a sharp investor, but also an astute insurer through the Berkshire Hattaway operations. Buffet has designed what he calls a "float equation", which provides an alternative way of presenting expression (5). According to Buffet, the return on equity of an insurance company can be stated as:[6]

$$r_k = \{((\ asset\ return1 - cost\ of\ float) \cdot leverage) + asset\ return2\ \} \qquad (6)$$

Where *asset return*1 is defined as the financial return generated by the investment of the technical reserves on the capital market and *asset return*2 is defined as the financial return generated by the investment of shareholders' paid-in equity on the capital market. The cost of float is defined as the underwriting result divided by the technical reserves, while leverage is defined as technical reserves divided by shareholders' paid-in capital. The only variation on expression (5) is that Buffet distinguishes two asset returns rather than a single one, r_a. This makes sense if one considers that the investment of technical reserves is, in most jurisdictions, heavily regulated (through allocation constraints, dispersion rules, currency congruence rules etc.) while the investment of the proceeds from shareholders (so-called *free assets*) is rarely regulated. The point Buffet tries to make with his cost-of-float model is that underwriting is key to the shareholders' value-creation or value-destruction process, especially as it is a highly-leveraged mechanism. This may explain why some troubled P/C insurance companies are tempted to recoup by "spicing up" the profile of their

---

[6] *Again, for time being, ignoring taxes.*

asset allocation. While such an approach may work once, it is (to continue the metaphor) more likely to be a recipe for disaster—preparing icing for a cake that is failing to rise! This may also explain why a lot of P/C insurance companies are afraid of seeing their business somehow "commoditized". Indeed, reducing the underwriting of insurance policies to the mere process of money borrowing (though, admittedly, a highly-structured way of "contingent" financing) is something that many P/C insurers do not like too much, even if it provides them with useful profit warning indicators. In fact, this borrowing analogy draws attention to a key strategic issue facing P/C insurers which can be illustrated as follows: when a policyholder is injured in a remote jungle, having taken out prior emergency assistance cover, he naturally expects to be repatriated as quickly as possible to a reliable hospital where he can be treated. In other words, he expects that, having paid his premium he will receive payment in kind, i.e. reimbursement appropriate to his needs—certainly not a cheque dropped by helicopter over the jungle! The same applies today to most P/C policyholders. What they usually expect is having their car repaired or their house fixed; they demand access to the best and most appropriate service with the least possible amount of hassle. In other words, like our unfortunate policyholder in the jungle, they want to be repaid in kind. An interesting challenge therefore presents itself to P/C insurers: How do they provide the methodology for this payment in kind? Do they become a selective contract network with car repair centres, hospitals, plumbers etc.? This managerial poser has, at the same time, become both more pressing, but potentially easier to solve, in today's on-line society.

After this short digression into the world of corporate policy, let us now return to Fairley's initial formulation for P/C insurance pricing. Simultaneous utilization of expressions (2), (3) and (5) enables us to come to Fairley's two fundamental conclusions, of which the first is an expression of the technical or underwriting beta coefficient (β_t) quantifying the sensitivity of underwriting results to overall market movements:

$$\beta_t = \beta_k - \beta_a(gs + 1) \tag{7}$$

As for the second result, it specifies the level of expected underwriting return M which would be compatible with conditions to ensure the equilibrium of the finance market:

$$M = -gr_f + \beta_t(r_m - r_f) \qquad (8)$$

This last expression shows that, in the absence of any anomalous rent, the technical margin hinges upon the risk-free interest rate (r_f) adjusted by the funds-generating coefficient and the undiversifiable risk associated with the underwriting activity (as measured by the second risk premium term). Let us suppose that €1 of insurance premium generates an average of €1 of investable technical reserves ($g = 1$), and that the β_t coefficient is nil (Biger and Kahane, 1978). Hence, the expected underwriting return is equal to "minus the risk-free rate". In other words, the expected underwriting loss reflects the interest rate credit for the use of policyholders' funds. This is an implicit interest rate (embedded into the rate-making), thus rewarding the policyholders for "lending" money to the insurance company. When the particular line of insurance business under consideration carries some systematic risk (β_t is not zero), the insurance company is rewarded by a risk premium commensurate with the systematic risk incurred. For example, one may assume that workers' compensation insurance is exposed to larger claims payments when the economy is growing at a fast pace, since the incidence of injury claims tends to become more frequent. Obviously this needs to be backed up by empirical evidence.

As stressed by Cummins (1988), Fairley's underwriting pricing model focuses on the underwriting systematic risk and overlooks a notion that is dear to actuaries, namely the probability of ruin. Indeed, one of the weaknesses of the CAPM is that it assumes the absence of such an outcome. As a result, insurance policies are priced as if they were free of default risk.

Nevertheless, the fact that Fairley's model rests on these assumptions should not prevent us from looking at its implications. Figure 1-2, drawn from Fairley's study, succinctly compares: (1) technical margins as predicted by the model; (2) those recommended by the Massachusetts Insurance Authority prior to the regulatory amendments; and (3) the margins as observed from 1966 through 1975.

It is striking to note that, consistent with the predictions of Fairley's model, the historical technical margins are negative and often close to their theoretical level of equilibrium. Indeed, it appears (as Webb, 1982 reminds us) that periods of vigorous competition on the insurance market compel companies to yield margin levels in compliance with the "1921 formula" in favour of convergence towards theoretical levels, i.e. those that are market-driven.

Line of insurance	Underwriting margins			
	(1) CAPM required margins	(2) Traditional target margins Massachusetts	(3) Historical margins	
			66–75	71–75
Auto bodily injury	−6.0	1.0	−5.6	−5.3
Auto property damage	−0.1	5.0	−1.6	−1.2
Homeowners	−0.3	6.0	−9.7	−0.4
Workers' compensation	−6.3	2.5	−2.3	−0.4

Figure 1-2   **Underwriting margins as expressed in premium percentage (Fairley (1979), p. 206)**

Understandably, Fairley's propositions have been the subject of much criticism. Some of this concerns the difficulties encountered in the practical implementation of the model and these are examined later in this chapter. Other criticism centres on the *CAPM* itself and, more specifically, on the crudely schematic vision of the world upon which it is based. There again, as the Massachusetts Supreme Court commented, the same basic argument could be formulated in opposition to any model:

"... we are mindful that the Commissioner's approach to the profit allowance is not only novel but complicated, and that somewhat greater imprecision must be tolerated in its initial application than might be acceptable in later years.

And although...the model may depart from the behavior of real-world companies, it is of the essence of the use of the model that it makes simplifying assumptions. The model is unrealisitic only in the sense that no actual insurer happens to conform its behaviour to the assumptions, not in the sense that its assumptions are fanciful or impossible to match in the real world." (Webb, 1982)

That said, it is necessary to recognize that some of the hypotheses put forward by the *CAPM* come across as more contestable in the framework of insurance markets. First, both insurers and the insured are somehow supposed to possess exactly the same foresight of the claims probability distribution (as there is no anti- or adverse-selection assumption). It is also implicitly assumed that the insured has no way of affecting this claims probability distribution (as there is no moral hazard assumption). Clearly, these assumptions represent an oversimplification, as confirmed by the large number of studies dealing with these phenomena (Ackerlof, 1970, Rothschid and Stiglitz, 1976, and many others). Unless insurance pricing and policy design involve proper remedies (e.g. deductible, *bonus malus* etc.), these discrepancies in information have the potential to undermine the quality of the company's underwriting portfolio.

Another contentious issue is the claims-probability distribution, which is supposed to comply with a normal distribution, one feature of which is a symmetry of distribution of claims costs around their statistical average. However, actuaries have long since taken note of the fact that a large number of risks (catastrophes, for instance) are characterized by strongly asymmetrical distributions, which are unlikely to be comprehended correctly through the dual parameters of "expected value" and "standard deviation". Notwithstanding that, the possibility remains of amending the traditional CAPM and thereby integrating this additional dimension.

Last but not least, Fairley's model fails to address problems arising from inflation, notwithstanding the fact that inflation quite clearly impacts upon companies' projected claims figures. Settlement of civil liability claims is highly time-consuming and is thus highly prone to inflationary factors. Once again, there is no reason why the basic model cannot be amended to address this shortcoming. Indeed, Kraus and Ross (1982) presented a revised version of Fairley's formula, which incorporated not only the previously-mentioned *underwriting* beta coefficient, but also an *inflation-adjusted* beta coefficient.

To be fair to the Massachusetts Insurance Authority,[7] these criticisms have not been ignored.

---

[7] *The new model has been implemented since 1982 for setting automobile insurance rates.*

To address some of the weaknesses of Fairley's model, Stewart Myers and Richard Cohn (1987) proposed a more accurate model based on the cornerstone principle of modern corporate finance—*cashflow discounting*. Myers and Cohn suggest that the funds-generating coefficient g is an awkward way of accounting for the time value of money. They prefer to account for it in the more orthodox fashion, hence the use of proper cashflow discounting (see Cummins, 1990). They dissect the insurance policy to its basic underlying cashflows over time. In addition, they incorporate a tax effect (which had thus far been neglected). The main objective of Myers and Cohn's model is to determine the fair level of insurance premium. To use Cummins's definition, "*the premium is defined as fair if the insurer is exactly indifferent between selling the policy and not selling it*". The basic formulation of the Myers and Cohn model is as follows:

$$P = PV(L + E) + PV(URT) + PV(IRT) \qquad (9)$$

Where PV represents the present value operator, P the insurance premium, L the losses, E the expenses, URT the tax generated on the underwriting result, and IRT the tax generated on the investment result. In other words, Myers and Cohn identify the various cashflows that will arise once the policy is underwritten. They take the policyholder's standpoint. First, the policyholder has to pay the premium P. Then, if a loss L occurs, it is indemnified to the policyholder. Policyholders are charged for the taxes incurred in the insurance operation. Indeed, the view is that shareholders back policyholders and assume risks by pledging their money. However, they could also acquire the same set of financial assets without having to incur these extra layers of taxation. Hence, the insurance premium has to reflect this. Once the respective cashflows are recognized, a set of proper discount rates has to be applied to each of them. This is where Myers and Cohn are close to Fairley. Indeed, one potential framework for computing the discount rates is provided by the CAPM. However, this is not the sole available methodology. Other asset pricing theories, such as the *Arbitrage Pricing Theory*, may also be used. Riskless cashflows,[8] such as insurance

---

[8] *In fact, Myers showed that the tax on investment income should also be discounted at the risk-free rate (see Derring, 1985, for a formal verification).*

premiums, are discounted at the risk-free rate, while risky cashflows (such as claims) are discounted at the proper risk-adjusted discount rate. The Myers and Cohn model corrects some of the deficiencies of the Fairley model. It is rooted in financial theory and, as such, avoids many pitfalls. Still, to be used efficiently, it requires the estimation of proper discount rates, an issue that is at the core of the Fairley model.

1.5   Difficulties in implementing Fairley's model

The main difficulty encountered in the practical application of Fairley's model lies in the determination of the technical or underwriting beta coefficient for each line of insurance that is required in calculation of the margin (see equation 7). Analogous with the estimation techniques used in determination of the beta coefficient for shares, the technical beta coefficients could be calculated by simply regressing, for a given time interval, the technical margins on the yield of an index representative of the market, that is to say:

$$m_{t,j} = \alpha t + \beta_t r_{m,j} + \varepsilon_{t,j} \qquad (10)$$

In which $m_{t,j}$ is the technical margin of the line considered over the period j, while $r_{m,j}$ is the yield for the market index obtained over the same period and $\varepsilon_{t,j}$ is a residual term of null average. Yet, for at least one reason, this procedure is not satisfactory.

Accounting statements provide the only available underwriting margin. To the extent to which it is based upon accountancy conventions,

	Underwriting beta	R^2
Fire insurance	0.002 (0.02)	0.00
Homeowners	0.056 (0.19)	0.00
Health insurance	−0.016 (−0.84)	0.04
Auto accident	0.119 (1.31)	0.10
Auto third party liability	0.059 (1.07)	0.07
Credit insurance	0.199 (0.32)	0.01

(Student t in parentheses)

Figure 1-3   Estimates of underwriting beta coefficients
(Biger and Kahane (1978), p. 130)

this margin does not necessarily reflect market opinion concerning the profitability of the line. Moreover, as Anderson (1971) and Weiss (1982) have demonstrated, companies have a pronounced tendency to "smooth out" their underwriting results by voluntarily overestimating or else underestimating their loss reserves. Under such conditions, one may easily understand how it is that the above-mentioned regression necessarily leads to estimated underwriting betas close to zero. Figure 1-3 should make this perfectly clear.

In order to circumvent these problems, Fairley (1979) and Hill and Modigliani (1981) have suggested utilization of equation (7), which again reads as follows:

$$\beta_t = \beta_k - \beta_a \, (gs + 1) \tag{11}$$

Their trick is to estimate the β_k coefficient of the insurance company's stock and the β_a coefficient of its portfolio of investments, and thence to derive an estimate for the underwriting beta β_t (as is the case for g and s, they are estimated on the basis of historical accountancy data). Even though this method represents an earnest attempt to align economic theory to market practice (with the exception of g and s), its drawbacks are too serious to pass by without mention. As demonstrated by Cummins and Harrington (1985), β_k is easy to estimate only when company shares are exchanged on a day-to-day basis on the stock market. It also so happens that it is difficult to calculate β_a, and, what is worse, it is only when annual results are available that this is in any way possible. Last, but by no means least, data concerning the portfolio of investments broken down by line of insurance are simply not available.

As for Cummins and Harrington (1985), they preferred to return to their initial method which they then rendered more sophisticated in order to take into account possible "smoothing out" of the results turned in by insurance companies. Figure 1-4 shows that the conclusions to their study may be summarized under three main points:

1) Contrary to the results reported by Biger and Kahane (1978), the technical beta coefficients obtained digress significantly from zero for a large number of companies, notably over the period April 1975–February 1981 throughout which they were all negative;

2) Results vary from one insurer to another and thereby undoubtedly reflect differences in both composition of the insurance portfolio and in the ratio of technical reserves/net worth;

3) The study is severely limited by its aggregate, rather than insurance line per insurance line, approach.

Company name	Technical beta coefficient *			
	1/70–3/75		4/75–2/81	
Aetna C&S	0.36	(1.70)	−1.60	(−2.99)
American General	0.45	(2.04)	−1.81	(−7.66)
Chubb	1.45	(4.15)	−0.57	(−3.41)
Continental	0.91	(6.92)	−1.64	(−4.57)
Crum & Forster	−0.05	(−0.13)	−0.79	(−4.22)
Framers	0.13	(0.46)	−0.66	(−1.57)
Government employees	0.13	(0.33)	−1.56	(−1.35)
INA	0.56	(2.31)	−0.55	(−4.73)
Kemper	0.95	(3.21)	−0.79	(−4.33)
Reliance	−0.35	(−1.21)	−0.80	(−4.89)
Safeco	0.38	(0.81)	−1.64	(−3.37)
St-Paul	0.92	(2.72)	−1.22	(−2.90)
USF&G	0.38	(1.78)	−1.56	(−7.21)
Moyenne	0.49		−1.18	

(Student t in parentheses)

Figure 1-4   **Estimates of underwriting beta coefficients taking into account the "smoothing out" of results**
(Cummins and Harrington (1985), pp. 29–30)

It is also worth mentioning that, whatever the methodology employed for underwriting beta coefficient estimates, the resultant margin of error is so substantial that utilization of the model for pricing purposes is to be undertaken with the utmost caution. It is to address these shortcomings that Michel and Norris (1982) proposed utilizing equation (11) drawn from Fairley (1979) in order to provide an adequate response to the following two questions:

- What periodicity for returns should be used when estimating the beta coefficient of a company's equity?
- What is the impact on insurance rate-making forecasts arising from the margin of error resulting from this estimate?

The first question does not break new ground, in that literature on the subject is profuse. We know, for example, that the systematic risk for a given stock is calculated via the regression of its returns on those of the market portfolio. Such returns may, of course, turn out to be daily, weekly, monthly—or even yearly. According to Carleton (1978) and Hasty and Fielitz (1975), selection of periodicity should hinge upon the user's "horizons". From the point of view of the Massachusetts Insurance Authority, the horizon is annual—insofar as review and revision of permitted technical margins takes place once a year. The calculation of the systematic risks of the shares held by insurance companies ought consequently to be founded upon annually-gathered data. As a matter of fact, Michel and Norris went out of their way to simulate no less than six time intervals (1, 2, 3, 4, 6 and 12 months).

In their attempt to respond to the second question, Michel and Norris set out by arbitrarily designating values for the parameters β_a, g, s and $(r_m - r_f)$. Using equations (8) and (11) as a basis, they determined three levels of theoretical margins. First, they introduced the estimate obtained for the beta coefficient pertaining to equities and then the two other values corresponding to the lower and upper limits of a 95% confidence interval (in keeping with the notion of "confidence interval" put forward by Stewart, 1984, p. 50). The results obtained, and summarized in Figure 1-5, show at first sight a sizeable difference between the minimum and maximum margins recommended by the model. Furthermore, and paradoxically, the observed differences grow as the measure of periodicity used in the return computation approaches the one-year time horizon envisaged by the regulatory authority.

Frequency	Minimum underwriting margin (1)	Mean underwriting margin	Maximum underwriting margin (2)	Diff. (1)–(2)
1 month	−14.3	−11.1	−7.9	6.4
2 months	−13.5	−9.2	−4.8	8.7
3 months	−13.9	−9.6	−5.3	8.6
4 months	−16.8	−10.0	−4.0	12.8
6 months	−19.5	−12.7	−5.8	13.7
12 months	−22.1	−12.2	−2.3	19.8

Figure 1-5   Underwriting margins resulting from a 5% margin of error in estimates of the stock beta coefficient (Michel and Norris (1982), p. 632)

1.6 First implications

The determination of a wholly accurate way of computing casualty insurance premiums is a major concern for actuaries. In their view, an insurance premium should reflect a mathematical expectation of claims payments, as well as certain loading factors. In point of fact, actuarial literature focuses on the calculation of just one specific loading factor, namely the risk factor (see Bühlmann, 1970 and Gerber, 1975). Even though diversified approaches have been suggested, actuaries nevertheless seem to be in agreement on at least one point: the risk factor must be strictly positive, so as to avoid insurance company bankruptcy.

The primary purpose of this chapter thus far has been to examine the compatibility of industry requirements with developments in modern capital market theory. The necessity of this type of research becomes clearer when we recall the fact that the determination of adequate insurance premium rates is not simply a problem for theorists, but equally involves regulatory authorities, investors and, obviously, policyholders. The American debate on this subject, lasting as it has since the 1920s, clearly demonstrates this. Nevertheless, in-depth examination of innovative pricing models, such as Fairley's (1979), has been both fruitful and highly educational.

The first conclusion from the examination concerns the role played by insurance companies' financial income in the ratemaking process. In the final analysis, the conclusion conveyed by theory is relatively straightforward: if a given insurance line carries no systematic risk , then the company will agree to post a negative underwriting result. Though straightforward, this conclusion may cause surprise because, to some extent, it invalidates the technical/financial dichotomy all too often invoked by insurers, and it recognizes the right of the insured to an implicit interest reflecting the outlay of funds for a more-or-less lengthy time interval.

The second conclusion is of equal importance, since it vitally concerns the adequate measurement of the risk factor. According to Fairley's model, the risk incurred by a given insurance line is correctly covered by the underwriting systematic risk. In other words, contrary to the assertions put forward in actuarial literature, the variance (or standard deviation) of claims distribution does not constitute an adequate tool for adequately measuring the risks taken on by the insurance industry *per se*. The risk factor derived by Fairley is an objective market-based factor wholly compatible with the existence of a competitive insurance market. So, too, is the Myers and Cohn approach.

It should go without saying that these conclusions are far from definitive and much effort is still being directed at the outstanding problems. For instance, the Casualty Actuarial Society has drawn up a Task Force on the Fair Value of Insurance Liabilities, and this has recently spawned a White Paper.[9] Meanwhile, the academic machine has not rested on its laurels. Following an upsurge in the use of options, and the associated boom in option pricing literature, numerous attempts have been made to investigate the potential use of derivatives pricing to address insurance rate-making issues.

1.7 Option-based insurance pricing models

In Chapter 6, we shall take a functional view of the insurance industry and look at the associated implications for the future of the industry. The basic premise is the recognition that an insurance policy is the functional equivalent of a put option. A put option is the right, but not the obligation, to sell an underlying asset at a pre-specified price (the *strike price*, or *exercise price*) over a given time horizon. In other words, a put option guarantees a minimum value to a given underlying asset. But this is exactly what an insurance policy does by providing an indemnity in case of a loss. Furthermore, Smith (1990) and Briys and Loubergé (1982) used this functional analogy in early attempts to use option pricing theory to price individual insurance policies. The same rationale can be used to build an underwriting pricing model at the insurance corporate level. Indeed, let us assume a simplified world with no tax. Two major claimholders are involved with the insurance company, i.e. the shareholders and the policyholders. To simplify matters even further, let us assume that the time horizon is limited to one period. In this setting, Doherty and Garven (1986) show that the present value of the claims held by shareholders E, and policyholders P, is given by:

$$E_1 = C(Y_1, L)$$
$$P = V(Y_1) - C(Y_1, L)$$

(12)

---

[9] *See the excellent website created by Makoto Okubo, http://www.insurance-finance.com, and the relevant sections therein.*

Where $V(Y_1)$ is the current market value of the insurance company's final cashflow Y_1. In turn, Y_1 is equal to $E_0 + P + r(E_0 + gP)$ where E_0 represents the initial paid-in equity by shareholders, and r represents the stochastic financial rate of return on invested assets; g is the usual funds-generating coefficient. The previous equation simply states that the final cashflow is equal to the initial cash amount grossed up by the investment proceeds. L represents the stochastic losses that the insurance company has agreed to indemnify, while $C(x, y)$ represents the current price of a call option on an asset worth x, with a strike price y.

The insurance premium P has to be such that shareholders receive a fair rate of return on their initial investment E_0. Hence, the fair insurance premium P^* is the implicit solution to the following fair-price equation:

$$E_0 = C(E_0 + P^* + r(E_0 + gP^*), L) \qquad (13)$$

The next step is to express the call option more formally. This is where Doherty and Garven are forced to make some specific assumptions regarding the stochastic processes of both the losses L and the financial rate of return r, as well as the set of investors' preferences. Indeed, contrary to traditional option pricing models that are preference-free (i.e. all underlying stochastic variables assumed to be freely tradable),[10] the model proposed by Doherty and Garven requires the specification of preferences. Indeed, insurance losses are not freely tradable and the traditional hedging argument à la Black-Scholes is thus not applicable. Cummins (1988) has expanded this model to yield risk-based insurance premiums for insurance guarantee funds. At this stage, it is fair to say that more work will be required if option pricing technology is to bestow its full benefits to the whole issue of fair insurance pricing.

---

[10] *Because the stochastic variables are freely tradable, a continuously rebalanced riskless portfolio can be constructed. This arbitrage portfolio avoids having to incorporate specific investors' preferences. They all agree to price the riskless portfolio at the riskless rate.*

1.8 New directions

The contribution of financial economics to property-casualty insurance pricing is highly valuable. Indeed, it helps to push the traditional actuarial approach towards a more focused market orientation, and this is especially timely given the current emphasis on the convergence of capital markets and insurance markets (see Chapter 6 for a detailed analysis on the current trends). One obvious consequence of the application of financial economics is illustrated by the numerous attempts to securitize insurance risks. However, there is one inherent weakness in the use of option pricing theory in the determination of fair insurance prices and that is the non-tradability of insurance risks. Nevertheless, the ongoing trend towards the securitization of insurance risks provides some interesting perspectives on this issue, as we shall see in the next chapter.

References

Ackerlof, G., "The Market for Lemons: Quality Uncertainty and the Market Mechanism", *Quarterly Journal of Economics*, Vol. 74 (1970), 488–500

Anderson, D.R., "Effects of Under and Overevaluation in Loss Reserves", *Journal of Risk and Insurance*, Vol. 98 (1971), 585–600

Arthur D. Little, "Prices and Profits in the Property-Liability Insurance Industry", New York, American Insurance Association (1967)

Biger, N. and Kahane, Y., "Risk Considerations in Insurance Ratemaking", *Journal of Risk and Insurance*, Vol. 45 (1978), 121–132

Briys, E., "Investment Portfolio Behavior of Non-Life Insurers: A Utility Analysis", *Insurance Mathematics and Economics*, Vol. 4 (1985), 93–98

Briys, E. and Husson, B., "Assurance Dommages: Haut-il s'inquièter des deficits techniques", *HEC Foundation* (1984)

Briys, E. and de Varenne, F., *The Fisherman and the Rhinoceros—How International Finance Shapes Everyday Life*, John Wiley & Sons (2000)

Briys, E. and Loubergé, H., "Le Contract d'"Assurance comme Option de Vente", *Finance* (1982)

Bühlmann, H., *The Mathematical Methods in Risk Theory*, Berlin, Springer Verlag (1970)

Carleton, W.T., "A Highly Personal Comment on the Use of the CAPM in Public Utility Rate Cases", *Financial Management* (Autumn 1978), 72–76

Cummins, J.D., "Capital Structure and Fair Profits in Property-Liability Insurance", Working Paper, *The Wharton School* (1988)

Cummins, J.D., "Multi-Period Discounted Cash Flow Ratemaking Models in Property-Liability Insurance", *Journal of Risk and Insurance*, Vol. 57 (1990) 79–109

Cummins, J.D. and Harrington, S., "Property-Liability Insurance Rate Regulation: Estimation of Underwriting Betas Using Quarterly Profit Data", *Journal of Risk and Insurance*, Vol. 52 (1985), 17–43

Cummins, J.D. and Lamm-Tennant, J., "Capital Structure and the Cost of Equity Capital in Property-Liability Insurance", *Insurance: Mathematics and Economics*, Vol. 15 (1994), 187–201

Derring, R.A., "The Effect of Federal Income Taxes on Investment Income in Property-Liability Ratemaking", *Massachusetts Rating Bureau* (1985)

Doherty, N.A. and Garven, J.R., "Price Regulation in Property-Liability Insurance: A Contingent Claims Approach", *Journal of Finance*, 41 (1986), 1031–1050

Fairley, W.B., "Investment Income and Profit Margins in Property-Liability Insurance: Theory and Empirical Results", *Bell Journal of Economics*, Vol. 10 (1979), 192–210

Fourastié, J., *L'Assurance au Point de Vue Économique et Social*, Payot (1946)

Gerber, H., *An Introduction to Mathematical Risk Theory*, Homewood (Illinois), Irwin (1975)

Hasty, J. and Fielitz, B., "Systematic Risk for Heterogeneous Time Horizons" *Journal of Finance* (1975), 659–673

Hill, R. and Modigliani, F., "The Massachusetts Model of Profit Regulation in Non-Life Insurance", paper submitted at the Massachusetts Automobile Insurance Rate Hearings, Boston (August 1981)

Husson, B., "Analyse Comparative de la Fonction d'Intermédiation Financière des Banques et des Entreprises d'Assurances", *Finance*, Vol. 5 (1984), 285–297

Kahane, Y., "The Theory of Insurance Risk Premiums", *Astin Bulletin* (1979), 223–239

Kraus, A. and Ross, S., "The Determinants of Fair Profits for the Property-Liability Insurance Firm", *Journal of Finance*, Vol. 37 (1982), 1015–1028

Lintner, J., "The Valuation of Risk Assets and the Selection of Risky Investments in Stock Portfolios and Capital Budgets", *Review of Economics and Statistics*, Vol. 47 (1965), 13–37

Massachusetts Automobile Rate Hearings, *Proceedings* (1975)

Michel, A. and Norris, J., "On the Determination of Appropriate Profit Margins in Insurance Industry Regulation", *Journal of Risk and Insurance* (1982), 628–633

Mossin, J., "Equilibrium in a Capital Asset Market", *Econometrica*, Vol. 34 (1966), 768–783

Myers, S.C. and Cohn, R., "Insurance Rate Regulation and the CAPM", Chapter 3 in Cummins, J.D. and Harrington, S.A. (eds), *Fair Rate of Return in Property-Liability Insurance*, Kluwer-Nijhoff Publishing, Boston (1987)

NCIC, *Proceedings: 1919*, J. Ferguson and Sons, Richmond (1922)

New Jersey Remand Case, *New Jersey Department of Insurance* (February 1972)

Rothschild, M. and Stiglitz, J., "Equilibrium in Competitive Insurance Markets: An Essay on the Economics of Imperfect Information", *Quarterly Journal of Economics*, no. 90 (1976), 629–649

Sharpe, W., "Capital Asset Prices: a Theory of Market Equilibrium under Conditions of Risk", *Journal of Finance*, Vol. 19 (1964), 425–442

Smith, C.W. Jr., "Applications of Option Pricing Analysis", in Smith, C.W. Jr. (Ed.), *The Modern Theory of Corporate Finance*, 2nd ed., New York: The McGraw-Hill Publishing Company (1990)

Stewart, J., *Understanding Econometrics*, Hutchinson (1984)

Valin, G., *Gestion des Entreprises d'Assurances: Mécanismes Économiques et Financiers*, Paris, Dunod (1984)

Webb, B.L., "Investment Income in Insurance Ratemaking", *Journal of Insurance Regulation*, Vol. 1 (1982), 46–76

Weiss, M., "A Multivariate Analysis of Automobile Insurance Loss Reserving Errors", Working Paper, *University of Pennsylvania* (1982)

Chapter 2

Securitizing Insurance Risks

Later in this book, we shall look back at the earliest instances of the use of insurance, to times when a mixture of prayer and earthly contract was used to mitigate the threat of natural disaster. Indeed, the arrival of Act-of-God bonds (see Favier, 1987)—an example of which is fully described in Chapter 6—marked the formal birth of written insurance contracts and structured finance, which were particularly well-suited to the risky business of sea-borne trade.

Here, we start by noting how these early attempts closely relate to current market developments affecting insurance risks. Investment instruments which are directly affected by the random pattern of natural hazards[1] are being increasingly traded, either on a standardized market or by private placement. In other words, physical (insurance) risks are being securitized and then placed to investors in the form of derivative securities or structured notes. In its most basic form, this form of securitization is exactly what the early commercial mariners were trying to achieve.

The Chicago Board of Trade has launched several derivative contracts in which insurance risks are the underlying assets. These contracts

---

[1] *Swiss Re Sigma distinguishes between natural catastrophes and man-made catastrophes. Natural catastrophes include flood, storm, earthquake, drought, cold, frost, hail, avalanche. Man-made catastrophes include major fires and explosions, aviation disasters, shipping disasters, road/rail disasters, mining disasters, collapse of buildings and bridges and so on.*

include not only catastrophic risks but also non-catastrophic risks, such as personal automobile collision or group healthcare. The over-the-counter financial markets feature sophisticated instruments, structured by investment banks such as Lehman Brothers, Goldman Sachs, Swiss Re New Markets or Merrill Lynch, in which the principal and/or coupons are partially/totally at insurance risk. In exchange, investors receive an extra return to compensate them for bearing the risk of losing money following an insurance event. Natural hazards that are potential candidates for securitization cover a quite large spectrum and include earthquakes, floods, hurricanes, aircraft crashes, hailstorms and so on. According to Swiss Re Sigma (1996), such bonds offer investors decisive advantages:

"In addition to providing an above-average yield potential, such instruments are attractive since their performance is not correlated with any other financial risks. They therefore promise an outstanding diversification effect."

It is interesting to observe that insurance-linked bonds (also called *insurance-linked securities*, or ILS) are often compared to corporate bonds. Indeed, investment banks use credits spreads on corporate bonds as benchmarks to measure the value implied by the spreads on insurance-linked bonds. The upshot of such comparisons is that these bonds offer outstanding risk-return characteristics. Indeed, it is widely accepted that, on the basis of historical analysis, an investment in an insurance-linked bond, after adjusting for risk, tends to outperform an investment in, say, Treasury bonds. For example, according to AIG Combined Risks, if an investment in natural catastrophe-linked bonds—with principal fully at risk—had been available over the last twenty-five years, its return would have been four times that of Treasury bonds with a lower volatility. A similar argument was applied in the 1980s to investment in junk bonds (see Altman, 1987 and Blume and Keim, 1987 and 1989). The fact of risk-adjusted performance, and the lack of correlation between natural hazards and financial risks, led Swiss Re (1996), and many investment houses, to conclude that *"this additional. . . possibility shifts the so-called efficient frontiers upward, within both national and international modeling framework"*. A similar shift was noted in connection with the introduction of emerging-market assets.

Finally, it should be emphasized that insurance-linked securities, when they relate to insurable hazards, enable investors to "play the insurance game" without having to bear the other risks associated with an investment in shares of an insurance company.

The purpose of this chapter is twofold: first, to unveil the structure of insurance-linked bonds and second, to revisit the case for their outstanding risk-return performance. Among other things, it will show that the methodological critique addressed by Ambarish and Subrahmanyam (1989) to performance studies of junk bonds equally applies to nature-linked bonds.

2.1 The origin and structure of nature-linked bonds

In his masterly piece on the history of climate since the year 1000, Le Roy Ladurie (1983) reports that 1316 was very wet, with some rather unexpected consequences. For example, the inhabitants of Tournai, a wealthy town of Belgium, were forced to drink their rather detestable local wine because heavy rainfall had ruined French vineyards! On a more serious note, though, it is clear that the financial consequences of adverse weather can be significant. For instance, a strong hailstorm can wreak havoc upon vehicle bodywork, mobile homes and roofing etc. Indeed, the fact that hailstones weighing more than a kilo have been recorded should leave one in no doubt about the potential damage they can cause. Of course, it is not just property that can suffer. In 1986, a violent hailstorm killed one hundred people and devastated more than 80,000 homes in central China while, in Bangladesh, a sudden hailstorm on 14 April 1986 claimed some 92 lives (see Gauthier, 1995).[2] Nature's catalogue of hazards is not confined to the tragically spectacular. Simpson (1997) noted that, during the period 1983–1988 in the United States, temperature variations in ten major population centres led the cost of energy consumed for space heating and cooling to vary by an average of $3.6 billion per year. For the country as a whole, the total variance was some $9 billion. This figure represents 12% of the $75 billion US market for heating and cooling energy demand. Natural gas and

---

[2] *Hailstones are not only a serious treat to people but also to aircraft. Indeed, on 4 April 1977, a DC9 was forced into an emergency landing on a highway of Georgia. Sixty-eight passengers were killed.*

heating oil distributors in the northeast area of the United States can have weather-driven demand account for more than 90% of their total winter season sales (see Simpson, 1997). In the United Kingdom, meanwhile, the last decade has seen subsidence risk come second only to gale damage in terms of costs to insurers. Although buildings are constructed with foundations that receive support from the ground itself, clay soil in particular is highly susceptible to drought shrinkage and consequent movement in those foundations—often leading to disastrous results for homeowners.

On the face of it, potential losses caused by natural disaster seem minute by comparison to daily fluctuations on the world's financial markets. Twenty basis points (bp) of fluctuation on the US financial markets is roughly equivalent to $US40 billion in value (Sigma, 1996), and this is significantly more than the size of the Kobe earthquake losses or UK subsidence claims. Nevertheless, while 20bp daily fluctuations on the financial markets are relatively frequent (unlike natural catastrophes), Canter, Cole and Sandor (1997) note that *"if a $50 billion catastrophe were to occur in the US, approximately 20% of the capital of the primary and reinsurance industries would be wiped out"*. Cutler and Zeckhauser (1996) make the same point. They argue, for instance, that *"while $10 billion is large relative to insurance markets, it is tiny relative to asset markets as a whole"*.

Such prosaic comparisons have recently led to the revival of the concept that alongside the traditional insurance and reinsurance markets, natural risks can also be priced and exchanged on the financial markets. The first proposal emanated from the Chicago Board of Trade (CBOT), where insurance futures contracts and options are now traded. OTC financial markets are also quite active. Numerous institutions, including investment banks, reinsurance companies and direct insurers, are currently developing insurance-linked assets as a specific new asset class. These assets are very similar, in both aim and methodology, to the very first medieval Act-of-God bonds. The most common assets in this new class are catastrophe-linked bonds.

It is interesting at this point to dissect a "typical" private placement (see Lehman Brothers, 1997). Let us consider an insurance company that wants to be insured against some catastrophe risk, in a particular geographic area, for a period of one year. Since the company is unable to locate suitable coverage from its usual sources (or perhaps it wishes to diversify its portfolio of coverage providers), it turns to an investment bank which suggests the following sequence of transactions:

The insurance company pays a premium to a so-called *Special Purpose Vehicle* (SPV).[3] The SPV then raises cash from investors. The insurance premium and the cash proceeds are then bundled together to purchase Treasury bonds. Having purchased these bonds, the SPV then issues a one-year insurance-linked bond, which yields an attractive spread over Treasury instruments. This bond is sold to the investors in exchange for their initial cash payment. As a result, the investors hold an insurance-linked investment and, in doing so, they accept the potential loss of part of the principal of the bond if some event (excessive winds, say, or an earthquake above a certain level on the Richter scale) occurs in the designated geographical area during the year, the exposure period.

If such an event did occur, the insurance company would receive its indemnity from the SPV. In turn, the SPV would be able to pay out this indemnity because it can liquidate the necessary amount of Treasury bonds that investors agreed to give up if the event occurred. The risk is thus passed on to the financial market. In this case, cashflows are reallocated back to where they are the most needed, i.e. to the insurance company. However, if nothing occurs during the exposure period, the investors get their money back and receive the Treasury yield, topped up by the invested proceeds from the insurance premium.

In a nutshell, an insurance-linked bond has all the appearance of a junk bond. A junk bond offers an attractive spread over Treasury investments because the holder grants the shareholders of the issuing company the option to walk away (usually when it is deep in-the-money). An insurance-linked bond could be described as a "natural" junk bond, where the investor is short of an option to reinsure the insurance company in case things go wrong. It should be clear by now that the whole process relies on the ability to ensure that the level of the insurance premium is high enough to warrant an attractive spread over Treasury bonds, and thus attract investors.[4]

---

[3] *The SPV is a shell that which receives the proceeds of the transaction. It is necessary, though, to make the insurance-linked bond "bankruptcy-remote". Indeed, the bond has to be contingent on the designated event only.*

[4] *For a full treatment of the pricing and risk analysis of insurance-linked bonds, see Briys et al (1998).*

2.2 Some caveats on insurance-linked bonds

Insurance-linked bonds are often benchmarked against Treasury bonds. They are described as superior investment opportunities much in the same way as junk bonds were compared to Treasury bonds. However, there are doubts about the validity of a straight comparison between an investment in insurance-linked bonds and an investment in Treasury bonds. Indeed, to be convincing, such a comparison demands that the respective performances be measured at the same risk level—and a true definition of risk is rather elusive. One common risk measure lies in the standard deviation of time-series returns. Guy Carpenter and Co. (1995) claims that that a 5% investment in insurance-linked assets increases the expected return of a 60:40 equity/bond portfolio by 1.25%, while decreasing its standard deviation by 0.25%. These figures should be viewed with extreme caution, since the relevance of such statistics is rather dubious in the case of insurance-linked assets, the returns of which are truncated. Indeed, the distribution of return on an insurance-linked bond is highly skewed. Once the triggerpoint is hit, the game is over. Hence, standard deviation is a rather poor risk measure to capture fully the true risk inherent to insurance-linked bonds.

Furthermore, when contemplating the prospect of investing in a nature-linked bond, an investor should be reminded that the past performance of such bonds is no indication of future performance. While this is obviously true of any asset, such a caveat is even stronger in the case of nature-linked bonds. One has to be extremely careful about the interpretation of comparative time-series sample statistics of realized returns on nature-linked bonds and Treasury bonds. The same point that Ambarish and Subrahmanyam (1989) raised about corporate bonds applies to nature-linked bonds. They showed that *"the time-series sample means and standard deviations (of returns on corporate bonds) would generally be poor estimators of the ex ante expected return and the standard deviations of return"*. This finding cast some doubt on the relevance of studies like Blume and Keim (1989), for instance. The reason for this result is that a corporate bond can be roughly duplicated by a portfolio which is long an otherwise equivalent default-free bond and short a put option to default. The time-series sample returns of a corporate bond are thus the time-series sample returns of a portfolio. However, the returns are not extracted from the same portfolio at each point in time. Indeed, the allocation of the portfolio between the default-free bond and the put option to default varies as time goes by. For example, the corporate bond can move from a AAA position (low weight of the put option to default) to a junk position (heavy weight of the put option to default). This in turn implies that the returns are drawn from a heterogeneous sample, namely from a highly non-stationary distribution of returns.

It is fairly easy to show that the same caveat should be borne in mind as far as insurance-linked bonds are concerned. A nature-linked bond can be viewed as a portfolio of two assets: a long position on an otherwise equivalent default-free bond and a short position on a binary option. The expected return on a nature-linked bond can be written as:

$$E(R_{D_0}) = \theta_P E(R_P) - \theta_D E(R_D) \tag{1}$$

where:

$E(R_{D_0})$ = the expected return on the nature-linked bond;
$E(R_P)$ = the expected return on the equivalent riskless bond;
$E(R_D)$ = the "expected return" on the binary option;
θ_P = the portfolio weight of the riskless bond;
θ_D = the portfolio weight of the binary option.

It is then obvious that these portfolio weights evolve stochastically over time. Consequently, in the same way the expected return on a corporate bond is highly non-stationary, the expected return on an insurance-linked bond is also highly non-stationary. The same holds true for the standard deviation of return which is beset by an identical problem. This implies that the investor will be confronted with significant difficulties when it comes to interpreting statistics on the supposed over-performance of insurance-linked bonds. In any case, it is misleading to draw conclusions on the superiority of insurance-linked bonds over Treasury bonds as long as the embedded "non-stationary" problem remains unsolved. At most, any claimed superiority should invite the investor to investigate carefully the sample path over which the research has been run.

2.3 Conclusion

Brealey and Myers (1995) define finance as *"a fun game to play, but hard to win"*, and there is no doubt that insurance-linked assets are indeed fascinating instruments. They enable investors to introduce a new class of risk in their portfolios and they demonstrate the endless ability of financial markets to engineer instruments that suitably reallocate cashflows across natural boundaries. The recent increase in natural disasters, and the surplus shortage in the insurance and reinsurance industry, cause these instruments to attract much attention. However, one should exercise great caution when dealing with nature-linked assets. Most recent studies are quite misleading and may lead the investor to conclude that insurance-linked assets are some kind of Holy Grail.

Nevertheless, these caveats clearly do not question the potential usefulness of nature-linked assets. Suffice to say that, since they allow risk to be spanned across natural financial boundaries, they undoubtedly improve the business of market participants and, in that sense, they draw potential insurance losses a step closer to tradability.

References

Altman, E.I., "The Anatomy of the High-Yield Bond Market", *Financial Analysts Journal* (July/August 1987)

Ambarish, R. and Subrahmanyam, M.G., "Default Risk and the Valuation of High-Yield Bonds: a Methodological Critique", Working Paper, Salomon Brothers Center for the Study of Financial Institutions, NYU (1989)

Blume, M.E. and Keim, D.B., "Lower-Grade Bonds: Their Risks and Returns", *Financial Analysts Journal* (July/August 1987)

Blume, M.E. and Keim, D.B., "Volatility Patterns of Fixed-Income Securities", Working Paper, Salomon Brothers Center for the Study of Financial Institutions, NYU (1989)

Brealey, R.A. and Myers, S.C., *Principles of Corporate Finance*, McGraw Hill, New York (1995)

Brys, E., Belalah, M., de Varenne, F. and Mai, H., *Options, Futures and Exotic Derivatives*, John Wiley & Sons (1998)

Canter, M.S., Cole, J.B. and Sandor, R.L., "Insurance Derivatives: A New Asset Class for the Capital Markets and a New Hedging Tool for the Insurance Industry", *Journal of Applied Corporate Finance*, vol. 10, no. 3, 69–83 (Autumn 1997)

Cutler, C. and Zeckhauser, R., "Reinsurance for Catastrophes and Cataclysms", Working Paper, Harvard University (1996)

Favier, J., *De l'Or et des Épices, Naissance de l'Homme d'Affaires au Moyen-Age*, Flammarion, Paris (1987)

Gauthier, Y., *Catastrophes Naturelles*, EXPLORA, Cité des Sciences et de l'Industrie, Pocket Sciences (1995)

Guy Carpenter & Co., (Kenneth Froot, Brian Murphy, Aaron Stern and Stephen Usher) *The Emerging Asset Class: Insurance Risk* (1995)

Lehman Brothers, *Introduction to Catastrophic-Linked Securities*, Lehman Brothers International Fixed Income Research (1997)

Le Roy Ladurie, E., *Histoire du Climat depuis l'An Mil*, Flammarion, Paris (1983)

Simpson, M., "Weather Derivatives: Shelter from the Storm?", *Energy and Power Risk Management*, vol. 1, no. 8 (Dec 1996/Jan 1997)

Swiss Re Sigma, *Natural Catastrophes and Major Losses in 1995: Decrease Compared to Previous Year, but Continually High Level of Losses since 1989*, Swiss Reinsurance Company, no. 2 (1996)

Swiss Re Sigma, *Insurance Derivatives and Securitization: New Hedging Perspectives for the US Catastrophe Insurance Market?*, Swiss Reinsurance Company, no. 5 (1996)

Chapter 3

Life Insurance in the United States: History of a Crisis

"I am not sure there are any serious issues confronting the life insurance industry these days, unless of course you consider solvency, liquidity, junk bonds, deteriorating mortgage and real estate portfolios, risk-based capital requirements, asset mix, separate accounts, credit risk, congressional inquiries, shrinking surplus, demutualization and more."

Salvatore R. Curiale
Superintendent of the New York State Insurance Department

3.1 Introduction

Snap judgements often make light of the facts. That, in essence, is the conclusion of Salvatore R. Curiale, superintendent of the New York State Insurance Department who, with great irony, states there are no serious problems in the life insurance industry—barring at least a dozen, that is.

The first worrying cracks in the American financial landscape date from the end of the 1970s, with the combined impact of deregulation, increased volatility and double-digit interest rates. During that period, competition underwent a structural change, as life insurance salespeople gained more authority, thus enabling them to negotiate the flexibility needed to attract savings more easily. They recklessly offered high yields and options, such guaranteed minimum rates, early surrender, contractual loans etc. The results were disastrous, with 19 bankruptcies in 1987, 40 in 1989 and 58 just one year later.

The substantial number of bankruptcies reflects the difficulties faced by *all* life insurance companies, irrespective of their size. Indeed, some very large life insurers, most notably Executive Life, were forced to file for protection from creditors under Chapter 11 of the US Bankruptcy Act. Thanks to an aggressive strategy, consisting of attractive product lines and large-scale investment in risky assets, this life insurance company was able to gain significant market share and grew from being merely a small company in the middle of the 1970s, to achieve the position of industry leader by the end of the 1980s. However, in January 1990, having announced high provisions for its bond portfolio, two-thirds of which comprised "junk bonds" (attractive, but highly risky assets), it was confronted with a wave of surrenders valued at over $4bn. In April 1991, the supervisory authorities of the State of California attached its assets and Executive Life achieved the unenviable status of the biggest single bankruptcy in US insurance history.

The object of this chapter is to provide an overview of the history of US life insurance and to explain the mechanism which led to its collapse and the ensuing debacle in the early 1990s. The chapter follows a broadly chronological structure: In Section 3.2, we look at the sources of the problem, notably the cut-throat competition between financial intermediaries to attract every marginal savings dollar, and biased regulation. In the following section, we see how the financial upheaval from 1979 to 1981 initiated a sea-change in the insurance sector, prompting American life companies not only to market new product lines by migrating toward interest rate sensitive products, but also to pursue much riskier investment strategies. In Section 3.4, we take a detailed look at the characteristics of the Executive Life bankruptcy. Finally, in the final section, we consider some of the conclusions and lessons that may be drawn from this uniquely American experience.

3.2 The source of the problem

In 1995, the US life insurance industry collected $339bn in premium income, compared with total assets under management of $2,143bn (see Figure 3-1). This number represents an aggregate of some 1,715 companies, and a total workforce of 2.3 million.

Year	Assets ($ million)	Premium receipts ($ million)
1950	64,020	8,189
1955	90,432	12,546
1960	119,576	17,365
1965	158,884	24,604
1970	207,254	36,767
1975	289,304	58,575
1980	479,210	92,624
1985	825,901	155,863
1990	1,408,208	264,010
1995	2,143,544	339,212

Figure 3-1   Life insurance in the United States (millions of US dollars)

Source: American Council of Life Insurance

The most salient change over the last fifty years has been the sharp decline in the market share of life insurers among American financial intermediaries. As Figure 3-2 shows, while the proportion of financial assets held by non-life insurers compared with other financial intermediaries has remained stable since 1950 (4% on average), the weight of life insurance fell from 21.1% in 1950 to 11.6% in 1990. This significant downturn occurred mainly in the 1960s and 1970s, years of bitter competition with pension funds. Since 1976, the market share of life insurers has hovered at about 12%. However, the fierce competition of the earlier decades lies at the root of many of the problems which appeared at the end of the 1980s.

	1952–55	1956–60	1961–65	1966–70	1971–75	1976–80	1981–85	1986–90
Life insurance companies	21.1	20.2	18.0	16.0	13.4	12.1	11.4	11.6
Fire & casualty companies	4.4	4.4	4.3	3.8	3.7	4.1	4.1	4.5
Commercial banks	47.2	40.8	37.1	37.5	39.2	37.9	34.8	30.9
Savings institutions	15.4	18.4	20.9	20.5	21.0	22.3	20.3	17.9
Pension funds	5.6	8.4	10.8	12.4	13.5	15.3	17.1	17.6
Mutual funds	1.4	2.3	3.3	3.9	2.8	2.3	5.8	9.0
Others	4.9	5.5	5.6	5.9	6.4	6.0	6.5	8.5

Figure 3-2   Share of assets managed by American financial intermediaries (%)

Source: Federal Reserve System

For many years, American life insurers stuck to a conservative financial investment policy. By the time the Second World War came to an end, about half of all assets were invested in American government securities. However, confronted with a demand for capital from private companies and growing home financing needs, life insurers gradually switched to corporate bonds and mortgage loans. By 1950, the asset portfolio comprised 25% American government securities, 38% corporate bonds, 25% home mortgage loans and only 3% equity. Around that time, bond investments had long maturities (typically 20 to 30 years), which seemed appropriate given the management horizon of the traditional contracts marketed by these companies. However, focus on long-term investments was not so much prompted by the wish to match long liabilities with long assets, but rather as a result of two decidedly more practical reasons:

- the rising term structure of interest rates and, therefore, higher long-term returns;

- the scant attention paid to the problem of liquidity, since net flows remained largely positive for life insurers.

Equity investments are historically low (see Figure 3-3). Perhaps this is unsurprising given that regulations on equity investment are extremely

Year	Bonds	Stocks	Mortgages	Real estate	Policy loans	Misc. assets
1950	61.5%	3.3%	25.1%	2.2%	3.8%	4.1%
1955	52.8%	4.0%	32.6%	2.9%	3.6%	4.1%
1960	19.0%	4.2%	34.9%	3.1%	4.4%	4.4%
1965	44.2%	5.7%	37.8%	3.0%	4.8%	4.5%
1970	40.6%	7.4%	35.9%	3.0%	7.8%	5.3%
1975	41.8%	9.7%	30.8%	3.3%	8.5%	5.9%
1980	44.4%	9.9%	27.4%	3.1%	8.6%	6.6%
1985	51.0%	9.4%	20.8%	3.5%	6.6%	8.7%
1990	56.4%	9.1%	19.2%	3.1%	4.4%	7.8%
1995	59.6%	17.3%	9.9%	2.4%	4.5%	6.2%

Figure 3-3   **Distribution of assets of US life insurance companies**

Source: American Council of Life Insurance

strict in many States. For instance, until 1951, life insurers in the State of New York (which had the biggest life insurance market) were barred from holding any equity investments. In 1951, equity investment was finally authorized, but only to a limit of 3% of assets. In 1957 and 1969, these limits were set at 5% and 10%, respectively. Since the beginning of the 1990s, however, US life insurance companies have been investing much larger amounts in equity, with a figure of 17.3% of assets recorded in 1995. As noted by Bollon and de Varenne (1997), this recent development has narrowed the gap between the industry standards in the American life insurance sector and those of its European counterparts.

In the 1950s, the life insurance industry posted high profits. These were boosted by the fact that the actual mortality rate was much lower than the actuarial rate used to set insurance rates; moreover, the interest rate trend encouraged bond investments. The only cloud in this otherwise sunny sky was the emergence in 1949 of the pension fund, a new savings outlet which was set to grow inexorably over the succeeding years. Initially, life insurance companies gradually introduced their own pension products. However, these suffered from a basic competitive drawback since, in contrast to the equity investment restrictions placed on life insurance companies, pension funds were entitled to invest in equity without restriction. Taking advantage of this, and the bullish stock market in the 1950s and 1960s, pension funds reported attractive returns. Life insurers, meanwhile, had to stick to a much more traditional portfolio structure (i.e. mostly bonds and mortgage loans, and very little equity). That said, they were entitled to offer contracts invested in equity—so-called *variable annuities* — provided these were denominated in accounts units.[1]

3.3 The financial upheaval from 1979 to 1981

Gart (1993) shows that the years from 1979 to 1981 were a watershed for the life insurance sector. Sharply higher interest rates, double-digit

---

[1] *These contracts are not expressed in currency units, but rather in units of account. Each account unit represents a fraction of one or more investment funds and the amount of commitment accepted by the company vis-à-vis the policyholder fluctuates according to changes in the investment funds. Accordingly, the policyholder incurs a capital risk on such contracts.*

inflation and increased volatility on the financial markets raised doubts about the future purchasing power of traditional life insurance policies; one way or another, policyholders wanted to take advantage of rising interest rates. This development had two major consequences for the industry: it forced life insurance companies both to redesign their product lines and to adopt a new investment strategy.

3.3.1 A new generation of life insurance products

Life insurance companies rapidly developed new lines of insurance products, notably policies pegged to changes on the financial markets—especially interest rate changes. These products shared two common denominators, namely guaranteed benefits and a share in investment returns (the latter being reflected in the premium and/or benefits). The array of products which emerged at this time included:

- guaranteed investment contracts (GIC);
- universal life contracts;
- variable life contracts (through which policyholders can choose the nature of their investment, i.e. equity, bond or money market rates);
- flexible premium variable life contracts (a combination of the two contracts immediately above).

The remarkable growth of single premium deferred annuities (SPDAs) also dates from this era.

Confronted with competition from other insurance companies (as well as other financial intermediaries, such as pension funds, savings institutions, commercial banks and mutual funds), and also under pressure from sales personnel, life insurance companies began to

Type of change	Type of risk	Characteristics	Examples
Lower rates	Decline in income	Financial income not enough to cover liabilities	Guaranteed rate Extension Policy loans
Higher rates	Capital losses on assets	Wave of surrenders Liquidity risk	Early surrenders Shorter contracts

Figure 3-4   Exposure of life insurance companies to interest rate risk

develop flexible solutions to attract additional savings dollars. In particular, these included strings of contractual options, such as yield guarantees, early surrender options, contractual loans, extensions etc. As noted by Briys and de Varenne (1997), these options—while being excellent marketing tools—have created additional risks for the insurers as they gradually deteriorate balance sheets (Figure 3-4).

This problem is particularly acute in the case of yield guarantees and early surrender options. Actually, most contracts offer a minimum interest guarantee and an early surrender clause tied to relatively low penalties. In case of a durable decline in rates, an insurer then faces the risk of reduced income—indeed, incomes may not be enough to meet minimum yield commitments. Conversely, in the case of a sudden rate hike, policyholders may be tempted to exercise their early surrender options in order to invest their savings elsewhere in optimum conditions and this can lead to a wave of surrenders—the much-feared *run* feared by insurers and banks alike. In such a scenario, insurers would be forced to sell their assets just after their market value had fallen.

Figure 3-5 shows the annual surrender rate since 1955. From an average of 6% in the 1960s, this rate rose to over 10% during the period

Year	Policies in force less than 2 years	Policies in force 2 years or more	All policies in force
1955	11.4%	2.5%	3.8%
1960	14.5%	3.7%	5.2%
1965	15.4%	3.5%	5.1%
1970	19.3%	3.9%	5.9%
1975	20.9%	4.5%	6.7%
1980	22.4%	5.8%	8.1%
1981	23.5%	6.6%	8.9%
1982	24.4%	7.6%	10.0%
1983	25.1%	8.6%	11.0%
1984	23.0%	9.6%	11.9%
1985	20.9%	10.3%	12.3%
1986	21.7%	9.0%	11.1%
1987	20.5%	8.3%	10.2%
1988	19.8%	7.0%	9.3%
1989	18.6%	6.7%	8.8%
1990	19.0%	6.6%	8.7%
1995	17.1%	5.4%	7.2%

Figure 3-5   Voluntary termination rate

Source: American Council of Life Insurance

from 1982 to 1987, peaking at 12.3% in 1985. These industry averages hide significant localized variations.

Another example of the potential risk emanating from the flexibility offered by this type of contract is the right of policyholders to use their contract as collateral in order to borrow from their insurers. Granted, such contractual loans have been offered for many years by life insurers, but large-scale applications can be dangerous for a company. In 1966, the interest rate on such loans ranged from 5% to 6%, depending on the relevant State. As interest rates rose, many policyholders used their borrowing option to invest their money at a higher rate and the average rate of contractual loans rose suddenly from 4% of free cashflow to 14%. In 1969, it amounted to about 20%. By contrast, from 9.3% of assets at the end of 1981, loans on insurance contracts dropped to no more than 4.5% in 1995 (see Figure 3-6).

Year	Amount ($ million)	Percentage of assets
1950	2,413	3.8%
1955	3,290	3.6%
1960	5,231	4.4%
1965	7,678	4.8%
1970	16,064	7.8%
1975	24,467	8.5%
1980	41,411	8.6%
1981	48,706	9.3%
1982	52,961	9.0%
1983	54,063	8.3%
1984	54,505	7.5%
1985	54,369	6.6%
1990	62,603	4.4%
1995	95,939	4.5%

Figure 3-6   Policy loans of US life insurance companies

Source: American Council of Life Insurance

3.3.2 A riskier investment strategy

In order to attract business, life insurance companies need to offer high yields and there are two basic ways to achieve this. The first is to use the term structure of interest rates: when the yield curve rises, insurers can invest in long maturities while, at the same time, the duration of their liabilities is significantly shortened by the introduction of greater flexibility. However, the discrepancy between the two creates a much greater interest rate risk. The second solution is to opt for lower asset quality since, broadly speaking, the higher the risk connected with an asset, the higher the potential yield.

This leads to the rapid creation of portfolios comprising riskier commercial mortgage loans and junk bonds. These two financial instruments offer higher yield in return for a higher default risk (principal and/or interest). As Figure 3-7 shows, with the exception of 1989–90, the period from 1977 to 1991 saw junk bonds more profitable than government securities.

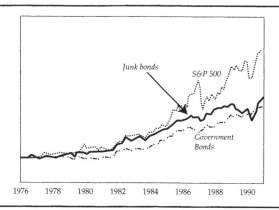

Figure 3-7   Trend of S&P 500, bond and junk bond indexes

Source: Blume, Keim

Some companies do not shy away from large-scale investment in such high-risk assets. As at 31 December 1991, the industry showed an average investment of 5% of assets in junk bonds and 17% of assets in mortgage loans (92% of which was in the form of commercial and office mortgages). At the same time, some individual companies were dangerously exposed to junk bonds compared with equity. These included Exceptional Producers (1,355%), Guarantee Security (1,355%), Executive Life (1,344%), Presidential Life (1,241%) and Investors Equity Life of Hawaii (1,217%). Others were highly exposed to non-performing mortgage loans: Chicago Metropolitan Mutual Assurance (506%), Supreme Life American (228%), Kentucky Central Life (162%), Travelers (124%) and UNUM Pension (115%).

Until the end of the 1980s, the junk bond and commercial mortgage loan markets proved highly attractive investment vehicles, with high average yield and little default. However, the first significant risks began to emerge in 1988 and 1989. Indeed, the onset of the recession at that time highlighted many difficulties. Figure 3-8 shows the mortgage loan default trend, which rose from 1.0% in 1989 to 6.4% in 1992.

Year	Rates	Year	Rates
1970	0.9%	1987	3.2%
1975	3.5%	1988	2.7%
1980	1.0%	1989	2.5%
1981	1.0%	1990	3.6%
1982	1.4%	1991	5.7%
1983	1.6%	1992	6.4%
1984	1.7%	1993	4.4%
1985	2.3%	1994	3.3%
1986	3.6%	1995	2.4%

Figure 3-8   Mortgage loan delinquency rates* in US life insurance companies

*Delinquent loans include those in the process of foreclosure.
Source: American Council of Life Insurance

Although the junk bond market hit a low at the end of 1990, the real estate market fell two-and-a-half times as much (see Figure 3-9).

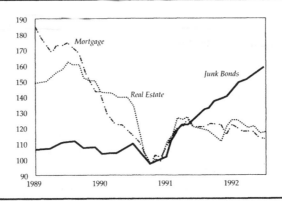

Figure 3-9   Trend of junk bond, mortgage loan and real estate markets

Source: Junk Bonds Composite Index (Merrill Lynch and Salomon Brothers), Wilshire Real Estate Securities Index, NAREIT Mortgage REIT Index (Base 100: 31 December 1990)

DeAngelo, DeAngelo and Gilson (1994) have calculated the cost of these high-risk investments for the life insurance sector. The total junk bond market ($205bn in 1989) fell by 9.2% ($19bn) at the end of 1990 and, for life insurers, the cost amounted to about $8bn.

In 1989, the office real estate market was estimated at $3,500bn. In a period of just 16 months, its value fell by around 30%, or $1,000bn, i.e. twice the value lost during the October 1987 crash on the New York Stock Exchange. Of the $3,500bn market total, life insurers held $256bn in mortgage loans and $47bn in real estate loans. In other words, the capital loss on the real estate market amounted to about $90bn for life insurers. From end-1989 to early-1991, the total capital loss on these two types of high-risk investment totalled $98bn.

The result was, of course, disastrous. Bankruptcies soared from fewer than 10 per year before 1987, to 42 in 1989, 41 in 1990 and 58 in 1991 (see Figure 3-10). There were several spectacular crashes: First Executive ($19bn in assets, including 65% invested in junk bonds), Mutual Benefit Life ($14bn, including 52% in real estate), First Capital ($10bn, including 39% in junk bonds), Baldwin United ($9bn) and Monarch Life ($4.5bn). This wave of bankruptcies can be attributed to a variety of causes, including heavy capital losses on junk bonds and mortgage loans, inadequate interest rates, non-liquid assets and a wave of surrenders. The public confidence crisis was further aggravated by the fact that the credit ratings of most insurers were lowered.

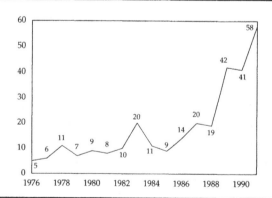

Figure 3-10   Number of bankruptcies of life insurance companies in the United States

Source: A.M. Best Company, Best's Insurance Management Reports

Since 1990, following a decade of heavy investment in high risk assets at a final cost of about $100bn, American life insurers have been gradually redressing their balance sheets. As Figure 3-11 shows, the average quality of the bond portfolio has significantly improved. In 1990, junk bonds accounted, on average, for 11.6% of bond portfolios but, by

1995, their weight had been reduced to about 5%. Moreover, the proportion of listed bonds, which are more liquid, has increased.

	1990	1991	1992	1993	1994	1995
High quality	88.4%	91.3%	92.6%	94.4%	94.7%	94.8%
• Class 1	66.7%	70.1%	71.0%	71.3%	71.9%	72.1%
• Class 2	21.7%	21.2%	21.6%	23.1%	22.8%	22.7%
Medium/low quality	11.6%	8.7%	7.4%	5.6%	5.3%	5.2%
• Class 3	4.6%	3.5%	3.1%	3.0%	3.2%	3.2%
• Class 4	4.7%	3.2%	2.6%	1.7%	1.6%	1.7%
• Class 5	1.8%	1.3%	1.1%	0.6%	0.3%	0.2%
• Class 6	0.5%	0.7%	0.6%	0.3%	0.2%	0.1%
Publicly traded	71.9%	73.5%	75.4%	76.9%	77.5%	78.0%
Privately traded	28.1%	26.5%	24.6%	23.1%	22.5%	22.0%

Figure 3-11   Distribution of bond portfolios of US life insurance companies by quality class*

*NAIC quality classes—junk bonds: Class 3 to Class 6
Source: American Council of Life Insurance

3.4 A typical example: Executive Life

Among the many bankruptcies in the US life insurance industry, the case of the Executive Life Insurance Company is rich in salutary lessons. Thanks to an aggressive strategy aimed at gaining market share, very attractive products and large-scale investment in junk bonds, this company became one of the biggest life insurers at the end of the 1980s. Yet, by April 1991, the supervisory authorities of the State of California had attached its assets. At the time, this was the biggest single bankruptcy in American insurance history.

Led by Chairman Fred Carr, Executive Life expanded rapidly between 1974 and 1988, rising from 355th to 15th position, in terms of assets under management. In 1988, *Fortune* magazine ranked it third in terms of profitability. When Executive Life was attached by the supervisory authorities, some 65% of its assets turned out to be invested in junk bonds (cf. an industry average of 6% to 7%), one of the biggest junk bond portfolios ever created. DeAngelo, DeAngelo and Gilson (1994) show that it is the high yield of this junk portfolio which enabled First Executive, the parent company, to pursue an aggressive marketing strategy and thus it is unsurprising that this bankruptcy was closely tied to the collapse of the junk bond market between July 1989 and December 1990. In addition to capital losses on its portfolio, Executive Life also faced a tidal wave of surrenders, about $4bn in a few months, at a time when junk bonds were in the doldrums following the announcement of a portfolio provision of $515m.

The case of Executive Life is unquestionably a landmark. First, it clearly shows the mechanism used by American life insurers to attract savings dollars in the 1980s, i.e. a willingness to take high risks both on liabilities (contracts sold) as well as assets (investments). When the risk strikes assets through capital losses on the portfolio, it affects liabilities through a deluge of surrenders. Second, this bankruptcy shows the magnifying role played by the press and brokers.

3.4.1 An extraordinary rise: 1974 to 1989

Created in 1962, the First Executive life insurance group ran into financial difficulties in the early 1970s. In 1974, Fred Carr was elected chairman and, under his guidance, its main subsidiary, Executive Life, was set to become the 15th largest US life insurer by 1988. (Already, by 1982, First Executive had become the third largest issuer of SPDAs.) Its products were mostly sold by independent brokers, who offered particularly high returns. This aggressive pricing strategy was based on a team of independent salespeople (to minimize distribution costs), as well as on massive investment in junk bonds. By the end of 1989, the portfolio of these high risk assets was valued at $11bn, of an estimated total market of $205bn. (When Executive Life was attached by the supervisory authorities in April 1991, they accounted for some 65% of the company's assets.)

By 1988, Fred Carr appeared to have achieved remarkable results: his company was the 15th largest life insurer, showing the highest profit/employee ratio and ranked third by return on equity. Until the end of 1989, Executive Life was assigned Standard & Poor's top rating (AAA) and the company outperformed the life insurance industry average. Figure 3-12 illustrates the main steps in the slide from stellar profits in the middle of the 1980s, to bankruptcy in the spring of 1991. In 1985 and 1986, the yield of the First Executive stock exceeded those of the life insurance sector, and the American market in general. However,

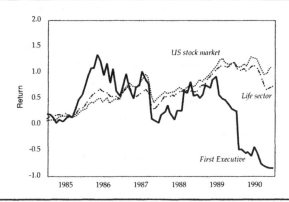

Figure 3-12   Stock market comparison

from the end of 1987 until early in 1989, First Executive stock actually underperformed the index, although it nevertheless matched the performance of other life insurance companies. In 1989, though, the stock price collapsed to well below the other two indices.

3.4.2 The dizzying fall from 1990 to April 1991

On 22 January 1990, Executive Life's stock price fell from $8.75 to $4, a drop of some 40.75%, following the announcement of a net provision of $615m for losses on the junk bond portfolio. In January 1990 alone, the stock fell 65.4%. First Executive revealed that its capital losses amounted to $968m in the fourth quarter of 1989, following losses of $528m in the third quarter. In the days that followed, Moody's, Standard & Poor's and A.M. Best all downgraded First Executive's rating. Ten days later, the regulators of the State of California installed permanent auditors at Executive Life and imposed heavy restrictions on management.[2]

News of the exceptional capital losses shook the confidence of policyholders. As Figure 3-13 shows, this lack of trust led to a wave of surrenders, which rose from $295m in 1986, to about $4bn in 1990—including $3bn in the first quarter alone. Some 70% of the surrendered contracts were SPDAs. Figure 3-14 summarizes the weekly reimbursements. Payments peaked in March 1990 which, given an

---

[2] *That is, restriction on the purchase/sale of junk bonds, reinsurance etc.*

Annual surrenders		Quarterly surrenders					
1986	295	1989	Q1	396	1990	Q1	1,698
1987	736		Q2	417		Q2	1,303
1988	750		Q3	208		Q3	439
1989	1,318		Q4	297		Q4	461
1990	3,888						

Figure 3-13   Annual and quarterly surrenders of First Executive (US$ millions)

Source: First Executive's 10-K and 10-Q filings

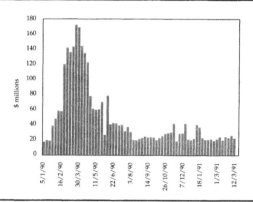

Figure 3-14   Weekly surrenders—Executive Life

Source: California Department of Insurance

average surrender processing time of 10 to 30 days, implies that the surrender wave started immediately following the provision announcement. Loss of confidence was so pronounced that, in February 1990, First Executive received an average of 25,000 phone calls a week from policyholders and agents.

On 1 April 1991, First Executive reported the results for 1991: a loss of $365m and a total capital loss of $2.6bn on its asset portfolio. The market value of equity became negative (–$2.5bn), which made the company technically insolvent. Its ratings were immediately lowered. On 11 April 1991, John Garamandi (the first insurance superintendent of the State of California to be elected by universal suffrage in January 1991) decided to attach Executive Life in order to prevent a further wave of surrenders and to end its insolvency. In the wake of this announcement, Executive Life of New York, First Executive's second subsidiary, was flooded by surrender requests, with the result that this subsidiary was also attached (on 16 April 1991, by the supervisory authorities of the State of New

York). Without its two main subsidiaries, First Executive was unable to meet its obligations and, on 13 May 1991, it filed for protection from creditors under Chapter 11 of the Bankruptcy Act.

The mechanism which led to the bankruptcy was typical: heavy losses on assets, loss of confidence among the public and a wave of surrenders. That said, in the case of Executive Life, the media and brokers also played a significant role. Indeed, several other life insurance companies were in similar difficulties at the end of the 1980s, owing to large-scale investments in real estate. The real estate market plummeted two-and-a-half times more than the junk bond market. Yet, by comparison to the spotlight which was thrown on Executive Life, the troubles of these other companies were largely ignored. The excessive focus on Executive Life was probably due to the US climate of opinion at the end of the 1980s, which had been galvanized by the collapse of the junk bond market, the downfall of the Drexel Burnham empire and the indictment of Michael Milken, the "founder" of junk bonds. Furthermore, since Executive Life had opted to use independent brokers to market its products, it not only achieved its aim of gaining market share but, ironically, also precipitated its own downfall. Faced with the company's announcement of enormous losses, brokers had few qualms about convincing clients to surrender their policies in order to place them with rival companies—and collecting fresh commissions in the process. Both magnifying factors, the media attention and the independent brokers, were of considerable importance in the case of Executive Life.

3.5 Conclusion

This life insurance crisis was not the first in the history of the United States, neither was it the only one of its kind in the world.

Indeed, it should not be assumed that the recent difficulties of American life insurers are a unique phenomenon in the history of insurance. During the Depression of the 1930s, insurers had already faced the impact of heavy capital losses on asset values, early surrender clauses and loans on policies. Their reaction at the time is of great interest. Dacey (1963) shows that about 40 life insurance companies (of the 300 in operation at the time) went bankrupt following the crash of 1929. In 1931 and 1932, one million policyholders hit by the recession used their surrender or loan options (for economic reasons, rather than to obtain better terms). In February 1933, faced with an increasing inability to meet their obligations, leading insurers decided to hold a meeting in New York. Also in attendance at this meeting (which was held in conditions of absolute secrecy) were representatives from the supervisory authorities, the commissioners of some 19 States. During this meeting, two radical measures were adopted:

- The insurers managed to convince the commissioners of the need to declare legal suspension of payment from March to September 1933, as had been done for banks. The main difference lay in the length of the standstill agreement: while the American government suspended banking payments for one week, insurers were given a six-month breathing space.

- The value of many securities held in asset portfolios had fallen to such an extent that many life insurance companies were forced to file for bankruptcy. The insurers' solution was to window-dress their balance sheets by changing the accounting rules. As a result, assets were no longer booked at market value (too low at the time) but rather at acquisition value (i.e. much higher).

Returning to the more recent crisis, the rest of the world has not been spared its effects. As Gordon Grant and Mike Lombardi[3] point out vividly, Canada was also hit:

> *"Take 145 life insurance companies of various sizes and strengths. Watch as a falling real estate market depresses profitability. Add the threat of major competition from the banks. Impose tougher regulation. And remove a few companies as their surplus shrivels up. This, in a nutshell, describes the travails of the Canadian life insurance industry over the last decade."*

At the request of consumer lobbies, the Canadian life insurance industry created CompCorp in 1991, a guarantee fund financed by the insurers themselves. One year after CompCorp's creation, Les Coopérants went bankrupt, soon followed by Sovereign Life and Confederation Life—the latter having some C$24bn in assets and holding the unenviable status of

---

[3] *Tillinghast-Towers Perrin, Emphasis.*

being the largest life insurance company to go bankrupt in North America. Europe was affected by the US bankruptcies and witnessed the slashing of ratings of the four leading Scandinavian insurers (from AA to BBB), the near-bankruptcy of GMF and the costly recapitalization of GAN in France. In Japan, the bankruptcy of Nissan Mutual Life, announced at the end of April 1997, confirmed that Japanese life insurers were also mere mortals. Of course, with 70% of its liabilities having a guaranteed yield of 5.5%, and with interest rates of 0.6% to 2.4% on the financial markets, the net worth of Nissan Mutual Life was bound to have naturally deteriorated. However, its loss is currently estimated at over $2bn.

The cost of the 190 American insurance bankruptcies listed by A.M. Best for the period from 1971 to 1991, in addition to the bankruptcies of US savings and loan (S&L) institutions—as well as other life insurance companies the world over—has been such that clients, shareholders and politicians are increasingly doubting the skill of managers and supervisory authorities. That said, several lessons can be learned from the American experience:

i) The mechanism which leads to the bankruptcy of life insurers varies little: competitive pressure between insurers, together with competition from other types of financial intermediary inevitably focuses efforts on premium income and market share. In turn, this leads to inadequately-priced products and larger promises to clients. In order to offer higher yields than the competition, and to meet promises which are underpriced (or not charged at all), insurers are subsequently forced to lower the quality of their investments. When return on assets becomes inadequate, equity is temporarily used as a safety net and, when equity can no longer cushion losses, a collapse is inevitable. Recent bankruptcies show that a company's size does not limit the risk of insolvency. On the contrary, the old catch-phrase "*too big to fail*" is clearly inapplicable to the life insurance industry.

ii) It has become clear that regulations are both inadequate and lax. This is clearly demonstrated by the case of the American S&L associations. The supervisory authorities, the FHLBB, tried to window-dress their balance sheets in order to prevent collapse and lax accounting rules were adopted. White (1991) shows the far-reaching impact of these changes: based on traditional Generally Accepted Accounting Principles (GAAP), 374 savings and loan institutions were made bankrupt in 1984 while, under the new Regulatory Accounting Principles (RAP), only 71 companies became insolvent. Rather than this attempt at window-dressing, the financial boil could have been lanced back in 1984 and, then, based on the market value of equity, it is estimated that the S&L crisis would have cost only $40bn. According to the latest estimates, however, the cost of bailing out this sector now exceeds $500bn. Until the beginning of the 1990s, US life insurance companies were not required to have minimum equity. The first solvency margin, known as the "risk-based capital ratio", which was geared to the risks taken with insurance assets (investments) and liabilities (commitments), was introduced in 1993. In Europe, the minimum solvency margin of life insurance companies is based on the third EU Life Insurance Directive which establishes a fixed percentage of commitments, and does not reflect the quality of assets and liabilities. The quality of insurance supervision has recently been called into question in Japan, too. For example, the chairman of Nissan Mutual Life acknowledged during a press conference that the net worth of his company had been negative for at least three to four years. Moreover, the supervisory authorities appear to have long been aware of the financial health of Nissan Mutual Life, but have kept mum in the hope that the conditions on the financial markets would improve. In reality, the reverse happened and losses have continued to mount as time has passed.[4] The supervisory authorities are therefore facing a daunting task in the years ahead: they will clearly need to adjust their perception of risks carried on the balance sheet of insurance companies and, most probably, change the traditional calculation of capital adequacy ratios. In common with the recent changes witnessed in the banking sector, the adoption of more sophisticated analytical methods, such as "value-at-risk", is inevitable.

iii) In exchange for premiums, life insurance companies book liabilities accepted *vis-à-vis* policyholders, i.e. promises they are obliged to respect. In the professional parlance of insurers, the producer is the party who writes the policy. However, the history of the US life insurance industry shows that the real producer of promises is the financier who needs to cook the relevant ingredients, i.e. the financial

---

[4] *For an analysis of the Japanese insurance industry, see Bollon and Brahin (1997).*

assets, chiefly derivatives, needed to guarantee successful completion of the insurance policy. These are the ingredients which end up in the investment portfolios of insurance companies. Basically, the financial markets provide the place where companies can obtain the financial assets needed to hedge, and hence to price, their promises. Adequate hedging of commitments amounts to a promise which is kept, i.e. proper control of production costs. This is why measurement and management of financial risks will gradually become the basic tools of a genuine growth strategy. More precisely, *Asset-Liability Management* (ALM) must be considered a management technique designed to meet commitments *vis-à-vis* policyholders and to protect the company's surplus, i.e. the market value of equity, against unexpected changes in the economic environment. (See the *ALM Survival Toolkit* in the Appendix.)

iv) Lastly, the American crisis highlights the role of shareholders in life insurance companies. The heads of insurance companies have long assumed that their business is less exposed than banking to financial risks. Indeed, they have been under the misapprehension that such risks had little connection with their core business. However, the failure to factor in such financial risks amounts to putting the company's equity in danger. In other words, poor liability management implies that the shareholders agree to make up for losses caused by adverse changes on the financial markets. It is clear that the prime interest of shareholders of life insurance companies does not lie in the changing fortunes of the financial markets—if that was their main investment focus, they would not need a life insurance company to achieve it! Moreover, it would be strange for the future of a company to hang on the unpredictable gyrations of financial variables, rather than to be in the safer hands of its talented managers. In the final analysis, insurers often argue that proper hedging is costly and likely to jeopardize competitiveness. However, this type of assertion reveals the pricing of insurance policies to be inadequate in the first place! The truth is not always palatable, but it is plainly obvious that insurers should not try to generate margins by speculating on the financial markets. They should rather charge policyholders for properly implementing the "insurance recipe", that is, for using the relevant hedging techniques. This is sound financial logic. By failing to use modern coverage techniques to control risks carried on the balance sheet, managers of insurance companies are guilty of focusing on policyholders at the expense of shareholders. Their strategy is to make shareholders pay for risks offered free of charge to policyholders on the dubious rationale that competition for the additional policyholder is fierce. Yet what market is more competitive than the shareholder market? Vigilant shareholders may dismiss poor management, but they are just as likely to take their assets elsewhere to a business or sector which is better managed!

References

Bollon, P. and de Varenne, F., "Assurance et Intermédiation Financière", from *Encyclopédie des Marchés Financiers*, 127–139, Economica (1997)

Briys, E. and de Varenne, F., "Assurance-vie et Risques Financiers: une Lecture Optionnelle", from *Encyclopédie des Marchés Financiers*, 166–185, Economica (1997)

Dacey, N.F., *What's Wrong with our Life Insurance?* (1963)

DeAngelo, H., DeAngelo, L. and Gilson, S.C., "The Collapse of First Executive Corporation Junk Bonds, Adverse Publicity, and the Run on the Bank Phenomenon", *Journal of Financial Economics*, 36, 287–336 (1994)

Gart, A., *Regulation, Deregulation, Reregulation*, John Wiley & Sons (1993)

White, L.J., "The Structure Conduct and Regulation of the Life Insurance Industry", in Kopcke R.W. and Randall, R.E. (Eds), *The Financial Condition and Regulation of Insurance Companies*, Federal Reserve Bank of Boston (1991)

Chapter 4

ALM in Insurance: An Empirical Wander Around Europe

4.1 Introduction

Equity performance, asset/liability management, hedging, subordinated debt, securitization... Over the past few years, the winds of change have blown globally across the insurance landscape. In the past, insurance companies had shown little appetite for adopting financial techniques to satisfy their shareholders. These days, however, the maximization of shareholders' wealth has become paramount. While some may attribute this trend to the pervasiveness and ever-increasing complexity of modern-day capitalism, others see it as a logical step in the necessary fight to preserve a resource, namely shareholders' equity, which, by its very nature, is the most onerous to maintain. Indeed, shareholders bear more risks than any other stakeholder in an insurance firm and, as a result, they demand a rate of return on their investment commensurate with that risk. Equity financing in an insurance company is clearly crucial, but it is also paradoxical. It is crucial as a safety-cushion, since it is the primary component of the solvency margin as defined by the regulatory authorities. However, it is also paradoxical to the extent that in a perfect world, where actuaries would be endowed with infallible foresight, there would be no need for insurance companies to post equity in the first place! Collected insurance premiums $(\ddot{a}_x)^1$ would

---

[1] For actuaries, "$\ddot{a}_x$" represents the expected present value—in other words, the premium—corresponding to a whole life annuity of 1 F to be paid in advance by an insured person whose age is x.

suffice to ensure claims payments. Of course, and perhaps fortuitously, this actuarial utopia has never existed. In other words, the expected value is not to be expected. Shareholders are compelled to commit initial capital to back up the underwriting of insurance policies and, in return, they expect their wealth to grow at their required risk-adjusted rate.

Among the array of risks capable of affecting the balance sheet of an insurance company, those arising from unexpected fluctuations in interest rates play a dominant role. A standard model of a life insurance company's balance sheet is presented in the next chapter.[2] However, the R^2 approach proposed here[3] is more pragmatic and, thus forms a useful introduction to the more complex issues explored later.

How do financial markets perceive the exposure of insurance companies to interest rate risks? Are there simple explanations for such perceptions? Are there any ways, if needed, to alter these perceptions? To answer these questions, R^2 is a very useful travelling companion as we take an empirical (econometric) wander around several prominent European stock markets. Whether or not one is an ardent supporter of capital markets, it is hard to ignore the transparency of the markets. This transparency, which makes the markets inherently efficient, relies upon the data gathering and interpretation efforts of a multitude of analysts and investors.

4.2 The perception of capital markets

When shareholders consider acquiring particular stocks, it is right and proper that they should do their utmost to become informed as to the nature and riskiness of their potential investment. Stock market analysts, who constantly monitor the risks of the stocks they are assigned to cover, are there to provide that information. In the case of insurance stock, though, how can one estimate the degree to which it is sensitive to interest rate fluctuations? Well, a simple empirical exercise can be performed and the way this is achieved is by reducing the stock of any

---

[2] *These kinds of models have been described in great detail by the authors (see References).*

[3] *R^2 measures the "adjustment quality" of a given regression. It quantifies the variance percentage of the dependent variable explained by the independent variables. In the case of a simple linear regression, R^2 means the square of the correlation coefficient between these two variables.*

Step 1
- Collection of a time-series of stock prices[4] and of domestic interest rates.[5]

Step 2
- Estimates of the slope coefficients of the following regression:

$$\text{Log } P(t) = a + b_s\, r_s(t) + b_m\, r_m(t) + b_l\, r_l(t) + \varepsilon(t)$$

with:

$P(t)$ = stock price as of time t

$r_s(t)$ = short-term interest rate as of time t

$r_m(t)$ = medium-term interest rate as of time t

$r_l(t)$ = long-term interest rate as of time t

$\varepsilon(t)$ = error term

The objective is to estimate the b coefficients specific to each rate.

Step 3
- Duration measurement (in Macaulay's sense)
  It is achieved through summing up the different b coefficients. This sum indeed effectively translates the response by stock prices to a uniform additive shock impacting upon all rates.[6] Quality of results[7] is gauged with the help of R^2.

Figure 4-1   Estimating the interest-rate sensitivity of insurance stock

[4] *For example, monthly stock quotes over a five-year time span.*

[5] *For example at short-, medium- and long-term rate over the same time span.*

[6] *Indeed, if δ represents an "additive" shock impacting upon the entire range of interest rates, Macaulay duration can be expressed as follows:*

$$\text{Duration} = -1/P*(d/P/d\,\delta) = -d/\text{Log}P)d\delta = -(b_s + b_m + b_l).$$

The multi-collinearity related to interest rates does not represent a real problem in this framework. Indeed, we are dealing with the sum of the coefficients and not with each of them per se.

[7] *Problems stemming from the presence of unitary roots and from the co-integration of variables have also been examined. But this goes beyond the scope of the present analysis.*

insurance company to a single dimension. More specifically, any stock can be converted into its "equivalent zero-coupon bond" counterpart. When this is done, the maturity of this equivalent bond, which is also its duration, can be used as a duration measure for the stock itself. The transformation is composed of three successive steps (see Figure 4-1).

Despite its simplified character, this method gives the advantage of offering a contrasting perspective of the varied situations of large-scale insurance companies within Euroland. For example, Figure 4-2 shows estimates of the duration of equity, over a five-year time span, of three leading European groups: Allianz, AXA and Generali.[8] There are some interesting lessons to be drawn, as we shall now discuss.

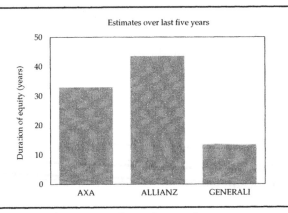

Figure 4-2   A European insurance mismatch snapshot

4.3 The French case

French companies, as typified by AXA, display a marked sensitivity to interest rate fluctuations. In particular, they are rather vulnerable to interest rate hikes. However, such a susceptibility is hardly astonishing because, first, life insurance policies issued by French companies embed many interest rate related options, including bonus options and surrender options (see the following chapter and the *ALM Survival Toolkit* in the Appendix). Second, the French life insurance market is

---

[8] *A more detailed study concerning the insurance companies quoted on the stock market taken as a whole is available from the authors.*

highly competitive and profit margins, if they exist at all, are very tight; as a result, many companies try to enhance their returns by investing in long-term bonds. The net result is a duration mismatch between assets and insurance liabilities (again, see the *ALM Toolkit* for more details). Their quest for greater returns is especially worthwhile when the interest rate curve is steep (i.e. long rates are greater than short rates), as it was so markedly during the period of rate convergence that preceded the advent of the euro.

However, there are potential pitfalls to such an aggressive asset policy and the year-end of 1994 serves as a good illustration of this. At that time, interest rates soared by some 150 basis points and the listed French insurance sector duly lost roughly 30% of its market capitalization, with a high number of insurance companies transgressing their minimum solvency margin requirements. There is no doubt that this is hardly what shareholders are looking for—after all, they can bet on interest rates themselves.

4.4 The German case

Michel Albert, former CEO of AGF, is often inclined to compare German capitalism with its Anglo-Saxon counterpart. In his view, the virtue of patience in the former contrasts markedly with the vice of "short-termist" stance of the latter. This view reflects the style of German corporate governance style by which cross-holdings are the rule rather than the exception. Anglo-Saxon capitalism, on the other hand, is market-driven.

Interestingly, this difference in style of governance is reflected in duration results. The average duration of German insurance stocks is markedly longer than that, say, of their Italian counterparts. The Allianz case, though, serves as something of a revelation—the parent company exhibits a longer stock duration than that of its subsidiary, Allianz Leben.[9] Were Allianz itself a mere holding company, owning shares both in life insurance and non-life insurance concerns, one would intuitively expect the duration of its shares to be shorter than that of Allianz Leben. Indeed, as we shall note later, the duration of P/C insurance stocks tends

---

[9] *Figures available from the authors upon request.*

to be quite short. Hence, the overall duration of a holding combining both life insurance shares and P/C insurance shares should be lower than that of its life insurance component. However, with Allianz, that is not the case at all. This is because Allianz is not a holding company in the strict (portfolio) sense of the term. Rather, it is an insurance company (and thus leveraged), the asset portfolio of which contains core investments in other mismatched financial institutions, such as Allianz Leben. The result is a mismatch snowballing effect. Indeed, the long duration of Allianz's core holdings is re-compounded by Allianz's own leverage. Thus, Michel Albert's observation that patience is a virtue of German capitalism should perhaps contain a rider to the effect that the cost of such a virtue is significant mismatching!

4.5 The Italian case

Italy comes across as a model student. The duration of Italian insurance companies' stocks, as typified by Generali, appears to be shorter than that of most European insurance companies. The truth is that the long-term end of the Italian yield curve tends to be rather illiquid. As a result, Italian insurance companies tend to invest in shorter assets, thereby reducing their asset-liability mismatch. It also true that, during the phase of lira convergence towards the euro, Italian insurance companies enjoyed significant capital gains on their bond portfolios. However, as the old adage says: "There's no such thing as free lunch". In this case, the apparent "bonanza" was offset by an increase in the value of liabilities!

4.6 What can be learned?

Looking back as these results, we can see that they are somewhat instructive, providing that is, they are viewed in the correct light.

In continental Europe, the liabilities of life insurance companies comprise contracts involving numerous "embedded options": these include a guaranteed rate provision, a bonus clause (otherwise known as profit sharing), a surrender option and, sometimes, a policy loan option (i.e. an option to borrow against the policy). Generally, the guaranteed rate is lower than market yields, while the bonus option makes up for the difference. The main asset holdings comprise government and other highly-rated bonds. Hence, at the risk of oversimplifying matters, an insurance company can be viewed as a large (wholesale) swap. It typically receives fixed flows from its assets (i.e. coupons from its government and corporate bonds) and pays its policyholders a combination of fixed and floating flows (i.e. the guaranteed rate plus bonus). Actuaries are utilized to compute a so-called "embedded value", which is deemed to measure the shareholders' value creation stemming from the issuance of insurance policies. This embedded value can also be thought of as the market value of the wholesale swap. If no counteraction is taken, one can expect that the market value of the swap, and hence the market capitalization of the insurance company, will exhibit a significant sensitivity to gyrations in the term structure of interest rates and asset prices.

This analogy with an interest rate swap also serves to indicate that many life insurers tend to overestimate the duration of their insurance liabilities. Indeed, actuaries value liabilities ($\ddot{a}_x$) by taking only the guaranteed rate into account. In the course of doing so, they overlook the bonus provision. In a nutshell, while they *should* compute the duration of a partially floating-rate liability, they actually carry on as if the liability was fixed rate.

The problem of overestimation of liability duration is also to be found in property-casualty insurance. Actuaries usually discount the projected nominal indemnity flows and then vary the discount rate to get a new valuation. Unfortunately, though, this computation is inappropriate, as it fails to deal explicitly with inflation. For example, let us suppose that interest rate fluctuations are largely due to unexpected shifts in inflation. In such a case, the actuary should re-estimate the nominal indemnity cashflows—indeed, their magnitude will change with shifts in inflation. Nominal interest rate movement will then be partially offset by nominal changes in indemnity cashflows. As a result, the actual duration of P/C liabilities turns out to be shorter than that usually computed by actuaries.

4.7 Should equity be covered?

R^2 appears to demonstrate that, to a great extent, insurance stock prices are inextricably linked to the roller-coaster of interest rates. But is this good news, or bad?

Unfortunately, there is no single definitive answer. It is of course possible to surmise what shareholders might say on the matter—and it is unlikely to be positive. They may, for example, argue that, as a vehicle for interest rate speculation, an insurance company is neither appropriate nor, indeed, handy! Furthermore, there are other instruments, including forwards, derivatives and bonds, that are specifically tailored to facilitate the monetization of interest rate views. Moreover, in bad times, they may criticize management for failing to resort to "just-in-time" capital, i.e. derivatives, to hedge unwanted interest rate exposure. Equity is just too precious and costly a commodity for its use to be debased.

Nevertheless, such views do not deter a large number of companies from abstaining from hedging under the pretext that its expense would render them markedly less competitive. In reality, of course, such an excuse is groundless. First, nothing is more expensive than equity financing itself. Second, as the French economist Frédéric Bastiat would have put it, what one sees conceals what one doesn't see. In this instance, what one doesn't see is the mispricing of insurance policies in the first place. Policyholders benefit from underpriced options. The cost of hedging reveals the cost of that pricing error. Is it thus reasonable to pursue a policy of selling at a loss and then trying to recoup that loss on the capital markets? It would be a bit of a long shot, to say the least, but there are some who no doubt place store in that old chestnut: "You have to speculate to accumulate!"

That said, the dilemma is not as hopeless as some would suggest. Financial engineering techniques developed by investment banks have something useful to contribute. The primary objective of any coverage of interest rate risk is to insulate the insurance company from the adverse effects of interest rate movements. That, in itself, is straightforward. However, as usual, the devil lies in the detail. Indeed, from the insurance company's standpoint, the burden of risk is not merely economic—the devil may well also reside in the accountancy, regulatory and fiscal details.

4.8 Factoring details into the insurance equation

We conclude this chapter by taking a closer look at these potential "devils within":

- The first is accountancy-related. The yield served out to those insured is a book-keeping yield and reduced interest rates do not necessarily lead to its immediate diminution. The need for coverage, therefore, is initially an accounting need, and yet a derivative product—a *floor*, for example—generates immediate payment on the same scale as the actual fall in rates. Most of the time this payment is markedly larger than it need be. Structuring efforts will be then required to end up with the proper cover and these may be effected in more ways than one (see the *ALM Survival Toolkit* in the Appendix). In addition to these constraints, there is another element that requires addressing, namely the mark-to-market issue versus the historical cost issue. Any accounting discrepancy between the object covered and its actual coverage cost is likely to incur perverse side effects.

• The second "devil" is regulatory and concerns the admissibility of the hedging products. It is akin to the accountancy devil insofar as it introduces the question of proper accounting for hedging devices. It also begs the question of what kind of statutory benefits the insurance company may benefit from by using hedging techniques. This is a significant issue and one which is discussed at European Union level. Notwithstanding the efforts developed in the so-called "Third European Insurance Directive", it seems that harmonization is not yet the name of the game. Many jurisdictions in Europe have yet to rule upon the admissibility of derivative products and this may appear a trifle incongruous at a time when prudence—not to mention a simple and urgent need—would seem to dictate the need for enabling insurance companies to buy back the options granted to policyholders. Another bone of contention revolves around the level of solvency margin (that insurance companies have to post) which, in contrast to common practice in the United States, is not readjusted to reflect balance-sheet risks. "Bad money" may well be repelling "good money".

• Last, but by no means least, the tax devil must be tamed. Indeed, taxation has the power to either foster or hinder the use of derivatives, and yet again, at European Union level, harmonization seems as distant as ever on this point.

These "devils within" are real, to the extent that they need to be exorcised if the industry is to survive and prosper. At present, they cost insurance companies in terms of both time and money, as accounting statements are endlessly tweaked to comply with an unharmonized, and somewhat unhelpful, regime. However, no matter how deep in the financial undergrowth, one should not lose sight of "proper" economics and that is precisely what the next chapter is all about.

References

Briys, E. and de Varenne, F., "Life Insurance in a Contingent Claims Framework: Pricing and Regulatory Implications", *The Geneva Papers on Risk and Insurance Theory*, vol. 19, no. 1 (June 1994), 53–72

Briys, E. and de Varenne, F., "On the Risk of Insurance Liabilities: Debunking some Common Pitfalls", *Journal of Risk and Insurance*, vol. 64, no. 4 (1997), 673–694

Cummins, J.D. and Santomero, A.M. (eds), *Changes in the Life Insurance Industry: Efficiency, Technology, and Risk Management*, Kluwer Academic Publishers, Norwell, MA, (1999)

Chapter 5

Life Insurance Pricing and the Measurement of the Duration of Liabilities

5.1 Introduction

The savings and loan debacle—with a soaring number of insolvencies of financial institutions—was a traumatic event for the United States. During the "Roaring Eighties", the US financial landscape was subjected to many changes, as rising interest rates in the early part of the decade led to a significant flow of consumer dollars into mutual funds. Competition for these savings became very fierce. This pressure, combined with regulatory errors (see White, 1991), had a perverse consequence for many financial institutions, as they reached for riskier assets offering higher yields and operated with increasingly less capital per dollar of assets. A good example of the effect of this refocusing can be seen in the life insurance industry, where companies found themselves forced by competition into redesigning their product lines and migrating toward interest-rate-sensitive products (see Wright, 1991, and Cummins and Santomero, 1999). The most obvious consequence of this shift to investment-orientated policies was a drastic change in investment practices within the companies themselves, as assets were restructured to search for higher yields, triggering a mismatch between assets and liabilities.

The result, as we know now, was disastrous. Prior to 1987, fewer than ten life insurance companies insolvencies had been recorded. However, in 1987 alone, some 19 companies went bankrupt. This figure jumped to no less than 40 in 1989, and on to a record 58 in 1991. Two particular companies, First Executive Corporation (with $19 billion in assets) and First Capital Holdings Corporation (with $10 billion in assets), were drowned by their portfolios of junk bonds, which represented more than 40% of their assets. Meanwhile, Baldwin United Corporation went bankrupt through mismanagement of its interest-rate exposure in SPDA liabilities. The insolvency of Monarch Life ($4.5 billion in assets), a leader in variable life, was directly attributable to its excessive concentration in high-risk real estate deals. Understandably, this very costly carnage prompted a huge wave of regulatory action. As the industry picked up the pieces, it became clear that much needed to be learned to avoid history repeating itself.

Across the Atlantic, Europe did not remain unscathed by these events. Although less publicity was given to the distress of some major European insurance companies, concern grew—and continues to grow today—among both European regulators and consumers. Indeed, as Figure 5-1 indicates, the major Scandinavian insurance companies went through troubled times in the early 1990s: most were downgraded, while others went bankrupt.

	1991 rating	1993 rating
Skandia	AA	BBB
Baltica	AA	BBB
Hafflia	AA	Failure
Topdanmark	A	BBB

Figure 5-1   Scandinavian insurers' ratings

Source: JP Morgan

According to an article published in *The Economist* (17 July 1993), many insurers in the United Kingdom appeared to become too vulnerable to sustain high "with profits" levels, with the result that bonuses were cut on these policies. In France, the 1990s also witnessed similar dynamics as in the United States, with the result that, these days, some 72% of French life insurance sales are represented by financially-orientated products. Needless to say, however, some French insurers have succumbed to the same temptations which proved the undoing of so many of their American counterparts—the failure of the Garantie Mutuelle des Fonctionnaires being a particularly costly example.

The objective of the chapter is to provide a better understanding of the driving forces behind a life insurance company's activities. In this respect, it is of paramount importance to understand the dynamics of assets and liabilities, since it is only through these that the riskiness of life insurance operations can be assessed. With this in mind, therefore, the crux of this article is a formal analysis of the balance sheet of a life insurance company.

Specifically, we consider four types of risk: asset risk, interest-rate risk, leverage risk, and default risk. To enable us to examine these risks, we require a model that is both utility-free and market-value based. Although market-value accounting is still subject to some debate (see Bernard, Merton and Palepu, 1993, Beaver, Datar and Wolfson, 1990 and White, 1991) and may arguably be difficult to put into practice, it is nevertheless far less misleading than the standard historical accounting approach. The model we use is based on Merton's contingent-claim approach to financial intermediaries (1977, 1978, 1990). An obvious advantage of the contingent-claim analysis is that it embodies the shareholders' option to walk away when things go wrong in their firm.[1] Only one type of life insurance policy is considered here. It is the most commonplace in France and contains merely a savings component and a single premium inflow. The rate to be served on the policy is fixed and guaranteed; however, regulation imposes an additional profit-sharing mechanism. Indeed, by law, French life insurers have to pay policyholders at least 85% of their net financial revenues—namely, dividends, coupons, realized capital gains, and so on.

To sum up, policyholders benefit from a guaranteed interest rate and a percentage of the performance of the company's asset portfolio. This profit-sharing mechanism is known in France under the name of *Participation aux bénéfices* and resembles British "with profits" policies. These British policies insure customers for a rather low basic sum, which is then topped up with discretionary bonuses (the profits), depending on how the insurer's investments perform. As a result, two key inputs characterize such policies—the guaranteed interest rate and the participation level. The model enables us to determine the fair interest rate, or the fair participation level, which policyholders should require to compensate them fully for the risks they face. The structure of the policy is thus spawned by the model, while the model as a whole is driven by a competitive market assumption, i.e. life insurance companies are both rate and participation level takers.

---

[1] *The application of option pricing to insurance avoids some problems encountered with CAPM—especially the effect of insolvency on the shareholders' fair rate of return (see Doherty and Garven, 1986 and D'Arcy and Doherty, 1988).*

As a corollary to the model, we also examine some current regulations dealing with rate ceilings, asset composition and capital ratios. We shall show that, in some cases, these regulations are either contradictory or actually redundant.

5.2 The model and its assumptions

We shall now consider a life insurance company, the planning horizon of which extends over a given time interval $[0, T]$.[2] Time $t = T$ can be considered as the time at which the company is subject to a comprehensive on-site audit by regulators. In the United States, these audits usually occur every three to five years. Their primary purpose is to assess the net worth of the life insurance company and to check that it is solvent. Indeed if, at the time of the audit, assets are found to be less than liabilities then the insurance company's assets are transferred to policyholders cost-free. If, on the other hand, the company's assets exceed liabilities, the company is allowed to pursue its operations uninterrupted. We thus ascribe a rather passive role to regulators like Cummins (1988) and Doherty and Garven (1986). They follow a simple intervention policy. In reality, though, regulators have a more active role and follow intervention rules that are more complex (see, for instance, Cummins, Harrington and Niehaus, 1993). The purpose of this chapter, however, is not to examine regulation *per se*, and we thus consider merely the simple rules.

Insurance and financial markets are assumed to be competitive. The life insurance company is a price-taker, and therefore it will have to service policyholders on a market basis. At time $t = 0$, the insurance company acquires an asset portfolio A_0 and finances this portfolio with paid-in capital E_0 and a homogeneous life insurance policy expiring at time T. L_0 denotes the premiums of this life insurance contract. If the company is not declared insolvent, new policies can be written for another period.

Only one type of life insurance policy is considered here. The closest example of such a policy on the US life insurance market is the Universal Life (UL) insurance contract that was introduced in 1979. The cash value

---

[2] *For a full description of the model, see Briys and de Varenne (1994, 1997).*

of a UL contract typically earns a minimum guaranteed rate of return. Some insurers then tie an extra return on UL insurance accumulations to the portfolio rate of return earned by the insurer. Some other US life insurers leave it to the Board of Directors to determine the rate credited on the UL contract. It is, however, fairly clear that this decision cannot really depart from the performance of the insurer's portfolio. It also corresponds to the UK "with profits" policies. This type of policy is also quite common in France. The first component of the rate to be served on these French policies is fixed and guaranteed. However, regulation imposes a profit-sharing mechanism, which is, as already mentioned, equal to at least 85% of the net financial revenues. As a result, two key inputs characterize such policies—the guaranteed interest rate and the participation level. The model enables one to determine the fair interest rate or the fair participation level policyholders should require to compensate them fully for the risks they face. In other words, the model yields the fair price of the insurance liabilities given the current structure of the company balance sheet. Based on this valuation, interest rate risk measures can be computed. These computations show, as already pointed out in the first section, that conventional wisdom needs to be "turned upside clown".

We do not consider the mortality issue, at least for two reasons. First, in France, these contracts do not carry any mortality component. They are pure savings vehicles. Second, introducing a mortality table would not change our results. As long as mortality rates are independent of interest rates, subsequent results (for instance, the duration measure) are not modified. It is, however, true that, all other things being equal, mortality cashflows would contribute to reduce duration. Indeed, cashflows may in that case occur sooner than expected.

The life insurance policy is structured as follows: the policyholder is guaranteed a fixed interest rate r^*. On top of this fixed interest rate, the policyholder is entitled to a share δ of the net financial revenues (dividends, net capital gains, coupons) of the life insurance company. As noted earlier, this policy is quite common in France and state regulation makes it compulsory for life insurance companies to pass on to policyholders at least 85% of their financial revenues (the *participation bénéficiaire*).

Brennan (1993) shows why, under specific assumptions, "with profits" insurance policies turn out to be inefficient. Indeed, a participating or "with profits" policy will be *"costly or inefficient in the sense that there will exist another policy that does not involve ratcheting and provides the same distribution of final wealth while requiring a lower investment"*. However, both Brennan (1993) and Merton (1989) account for the existence of such policies by arguing that transaction costs provide a reason for financial intermediation. The insurance contract can then be viewed as a product that is not directly available on the market and thus, by issuing such a contract, the insurance company actually contributes to a more complete market.

Note that the regulation of the participation level in France dates back to 1966, at a time when insurees were still mindful of the poor post-war performance of their life insurance policies—which were not protected against inflation. It is for that reason that regulators chose to introduce a form of indexation through the *participation bénéficiaire*.

Thus, the company is obliged to tell policyholders the fraction δ ($\delta \geq$ 85%) that it is going to distribute to them. Although regulators claim that inflation is the origin of the participation mechanism, there is another way of rationalizing it.

The guaranteed rate r^* is usually less than the market rate for a risk-free asset of the same maturity as the policy. The participation coefficient δ can be viewed as making up for the difference between the two rates and embodying the required risk premium of policyholders holding risky life insurance policies. Indeed, shareholders have a limited liability and, if the company is declared insolvent at time $t = T$, they simply walk away. Under such a scenario, policyholders receive only what is left.[3] As the model is developed, this aspect becomes quite clear.

It is assumed in this chapter that the life insurance company is owned by shareholders who have a limited liability. Another way to organize a life insurance concern is by way of a mutual company, where the policyholders are also the owners of the company. But in that case, however, policyholders of mutuals have limited liability with respect to their ownership interest in the mutual. With respect to their loss payment claims against the insurer, the policyholders stand in the same role as policyholders of stock companies.

At time $t = 0$, the company's balance sheet appears as shown in Figure 5-2. For the sake of simplicity, we normalize A_0 to the value of one dollar.

---

[3] *Ingersoll (1987) explains why the policyholders have no incentive to renegotiate their contracts in case of default.*

Assets		Liabilities and equity	
Assets	A_0	Liabilities	$L_0 = \alpha A_0$
		Equity	$E_0 = (1-\alpha)A_0$
Total	A_0	Total	A_0

Figure 5-2   The company's balance sheet at time $t = 0$

Then $(1-\alpha)$ denotes the proportion of the initial assets A_0 financed by equity. This is a decision-variable of the company. The initial portfolio of assets is assumed to be totally invested in risky assets (equity, risky bonds, real estate).

The first risk element of the balance sheet is interest-rate risk. To capture the uncertainty in the term structure of interest rates, the short-term interest rates are assumed to be normally distributed and to follow an Ornstein-Uhlenbeck process. In such a framework, which corresponds to the Vasicek (1977) model,[4] the short-term riskless interest rate r_t dynamics are given at time t by the following stochastic differential equation:

$$dr_t = a[b - r_t]dt + \sigma dW_t \tag{1}$$

where a, b and σ are positive constant parameters. σ is the instantaneous standard deviation of r_t. W_t is a standard Brownian motion. According to (1) the dynamics of return of the default-free zero-coupon bond $P(t, T)$ maturing at time T is given at time t by:

$$\frac{dP(t, T)}{P(t, T)} = r_t dt - \sigma_P(T - t)dW_t \tag{2}$$

where $\sigma_P(t, T)$ is a deterministic function defined by:

---

[4] *The only drawback is that negative interest rates are not precluded in a gaussian environment. Nevertheless, it should be noted that for reasonable values of the parameters, this event has a quite low probability of occurrence.*

$$\sigma_P (t, T) = \frac{\sigma}{a} \cdot (1 - e^{-a(T-t)}) \tag{3}$$

Vasicek (1977) shows that the value of $P(t, T)$ is a function of both the instantaneous riskless interest rate r_t and the time-to-maturity $(T-t)$ of the bond and can be stated as:

$$P(t, T) = G(T - t) \cdot \exp(-H(T - t)r_t) \tag{4}$$

with:

$$H(T - t) = \frac{1 - e^{-a(T-t)}}{a}$$

$$G(T-t) = \exp\left[\left(\frac{\sigma^2}{2a^2} - b\right)(T-t) + \left(b - \frac{\sigma^2}{a^2}\right)H(T-t) + \frac{\sigma^2}{4a^2}H(2(T-t))\right]$$

The second risk element is asset risk—that is, all risk-affecting assets (equity, real estate) other than the interest-rate risk. To give a complete picture of the riskiness of the insurance company, the portfolio of assets is assumed to be affected by both the interest-rate risk and the asset risk.

As a result, the portfolio of assets A_t is assumed to be governed by the following stochastic process:

$$\frac{dA_t}{A_t} = \mu dt + \sigma_A \left[\rho dW_t + \sqrt{1 - \rho^2}\, dZ_t\right] \tag{5}$$

where μ and σ_A denote, respectively, the instantaneous expected return on assets and their instantaneous volatility. Z_t is a standard Wiener process independent of W_t capturing the asset risk other than the interest-rate risk. The coefficient ρ, included between -1 and $+1$, represents the correlation between the total value of assets A_t and the interest rate r_t. In other words, ρ corresponds to the share of interest-rate risk in the total risk of the assets. More specifically, the total variance of assets σ_A^2 can be split into two parts: an interest-rate risk component $\rho^2\sigma_A^2$ and an asset-risk component $(1-\rho^2)\sigma_A^2$.

We define the financial bonus B_T to policyholders once guaranteed payments have been cashed out as of time T by the following positive amount:

$$B_T = \max\left[0, \delta\left(\frac{L_0}{A_0}(A_T - A_0) - (L_T^* - L_0)\right)\right]$$

$$= \delta\alpha \max\left[0, A_T - \frac{L_T^*}{\alpha}\right]$$

(6)

where $L_T^* = L_0 e^{r^*T}$ is the time T guaranteed payment to policyholders. Indeed, the total financial revenues $(A_T - A_0)$ of the company between $t = 0$ and $t = T$ are assumed to be earmarked so that only a fraction $L_0/A_0 = \alpha$ of them are taken into account for the policyholders' bonus. After guaranteed commitments $(L_T^* - L_0)$ have been fulfilled and deducted from the financial profits, policyholders receive a share δ of these net financial revenues. The insurance company starts to share its profits as soon as B_T is positive, namely when $A_T \geq L_T^*/\alpha$. In other words, because $L_T^*/\alpha = A_0 e^{r^*T}$, the company begins to serve a bonus as soon as the rate of return on the assets is bigger than the guaranteed interest rate r^*.

Under this setting and using the contractual definition of stakeholders' cashflows, one can write the policyholders' payoffs L_T at maturity as follows. Three states of nature have to be clearly distinguished.

1 In the first scenario (the worst case scenario), the insurer is totally insolvent: $A_T < L_T^*$. The time T value of assets is below the guaranteed liability. The company is then declared bankrupt, and the policyholders receive what is left:

$$L_T = A_T \quad \text{if } A_T < L_T^*$$

(7)

2 In the second case, the company is able to fulfil its guaranteed commitment, but unable to serve the bonus $(B_T = 0)$.

$$L_T = L_T^* \quad \text{if } L_T^* \leq A_T < \frac{L_T^*}{\alpha} \tag{8}$$

3 In the third case, the bonus B_T is positive or $A_T \geq \frac{L_T^*}{\alpha}$. Assets generate enough value to match the guaranteed payment and the policyholders' participation. In such a case, the liabilities at time T are equal to:

$$L_T = L_T^* + B_T \quad \text{if } \frac{L_T^*}{\alpha} \leq A_T$$
$$= \delta \alpha A_T + (1 - \delta) L_T^* \tag{9}$$

To sum up, the first case corresponds to a case of total insolvency; the second case is a partial insolvency (in the sense that only guaranteed commitments are fulfilled) and the third case corresponds to a fully-solvent scenario.

The value L_T^*/α delimiting the third case is not innocuous. Indeed, with our notation,

$$\frac{L_T^*}{\alpha} = \frac{L_0 e^{r^* T}}{L_0/A_0} = A_0 e^{r^* T} \tag{10}$$

the company starts to share its profits as soon as the rate of return on the assets is larger than the guaranteed interest rate r^*.

Due to limited liability, the shareholders' stake is a residual stake. The final payoffs E_T are therefore as follows:

First case: $E_T = 0$ if $A_T < L_T^*$

Second case: $E_T = A_T - L_T^*$ if $L_T^* \leq A_T < \frac{L_T^*}{\alpha}$

Third case: $E_T = (1 - \delta \alpha) A_T - (1 - \delta) L_T^*$ if $\frac{L_T^*}{\alpha} \leq A_T$

These payoffs suggest that equity and liabilities have the features of contingent claims written on the insurance company's assets and, indeed, cashflows are truncated. Since the seminal works of Black and Scholes (1973) and Merton (1973), it is widely accepted that the limited liability equity of a leveraged firm can be valued as a contingent claim on the firm's underlying assets. The only difference here is that the contractual structure is more involved and includes features that are not present in the simplified picture à la Black-Scholes-Merton.

5.3   Equity and liabilities valuation

By applying the option pricing framework (see Merton, 1990, Ronn and Verma, 1986 and Crouhy and Galai, 1991), the market value of both equity and liabilities can be assessed. As far as equity is concerned, Section 5.2 indicates that the value of equity as of time T is given by:

$$E_T = \max[0, A_T - L_T^*] - \delta\alpha \max\left[0, A_T - \frac{L_T^*}{\alpha}\right] \qquad (11)$$

The two terms on the right-hand side are nothing but the final payoffs on two call options maturing at time T, with exercise prices L_T^* and L_T^*/α. The value of equity at time t can thus be rewritten as:

$$E_t = C_E(A_t, L_T^*) - \delta\alpha C_E(A_t, \frac{L_T^*}{\alpha}) \qquad (12)$$

where $C_E(A_t, L_T^*)$, and $C_E(A_t, L_T^*/\alpha)$ are both European calls maturing at time $T - t$ and with exercise prices L_T^* and L_T^*/α.

$$C_E(A_t, L_T^*) = A_t N(d_1) - P(t, T)L_T^* N(d_2)$$
$$C_E(A_t, \frac{L_T^*}{\alpha}) = A_t N(d_3) - P(t, T)\frac{L_T^*}{\alpha} N(d_4) \qquad (13)$$

with

$$d_1 = \frac{\ln A_t / P(t, T)L_T^* + \bar{\sigma}(t, T)^2(T - t)/2}{\bar{\sigma}(t, T)\sqrt{(T - t)}} = d_2 + \bar{\sigma}(t, T)\sqrt{(T - t)}$$

$$d_4 = \frac{\ln\alpha\, A_t / P(t,T)L_T^* + \bar{\sigma}(t,T)^2(T-t)/2}{\bar{\sigma}(t,T)\sqrt{(T-t)}} = d_4 + \bar{\sigma}(t,T)\sqrt{(T-t)}$$

$$\bar{\sigma}(t,T)^2 = \frac{1}{T-t}\cdot\int_t^T [(\rho\sigma_A + \sigma_P(u,T))^2 + (1-\rho^2)\sigma_A^2]\,du$$

$N(\ ) = $ the cumulative normal distribution

With (13), equation (12) becomes

$$E_t = A_t[N(d_1) - \delta\alpha N(d_3)] - P(t,T)L_T^*[N(d_2) - \delta N(d_4)] \qquad (14)$$

The equity of the life insurance company is a hybrid entity, a portfolio of two European calls. The first term on the right-hand side of expression (12) is easy to understand. Indeed, if one let δ equal to zero, this first term is the familiar limited liability call option.[5] Shareholders have the option to walk away if things go wrong. The second term appears because of the potential bonus. This term is also a call option. A bonus is equivalent for the policyholders to having a call option on the performance of the insurance company assets. Equity is thus made of a long (limited liability) call position and a short call position, the latter being weighted by the bonus level δ, as well as α. Figure 5-3 pictures the cashflow position of the company's shareholders at time T.

As far as liabilities are concerned, the final payoffs in Section 5.2 indicate that they can be priced as follows:

$$L_t = L_T^* P(t,T) - P_E(A_t, L_T^*) + \delta\alpha C_E\left(A_t, \frac{L_T^*}{\alpha}\right) \qquad (15)$$

where $P_E(A_t, L_T^*)$ denotes the price of the shareholders' put to default—that is, the right to walk away from their guaranteed commitments:

[5] *See Black and Scholes (1973) and Merton (1973).*

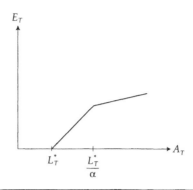

Figure 5-3   Shareholders' final payoffs

The liabilities are thus made of a long position on a risk-free payoff, a short position on a put to default, and a long position on a call on financial revenues. More specifically, the first two terms in (15) represent the value of a risky policy without participation (that is, a risky bond). The third term is a call option on a fraction of the firm with the exercise price L_T^*.

$$P_E\,(A_t\,,L_T^*)=-A_t\,N\,(-d_1)+P\,(t,T)\,L_T^*\,N(-d_2) \qquad (16)$$

Using the formula for the European put, equation (16) can be written as follows:

$$L_t = A_t\,[N(-d_1)+\delta\alpha N\,(d_3)]+P\,(t,T)\,L_T^*\,[N(d_2)-\delta N(d_4)] \qquad (17)$$

This combined position can be summarized by Figure 5-4, which shows liability cashflows as of time T.

From equations (12) and (15), we can see that the relevant volatility parameter for pricing both equity and liabilities is $\bar{\sigma}\,(t,T)$ which represents the volatility of the ratio $A_t/P\,(t,T)$ or, in other words, the volatility of the firm's assets using the default-free zero-coupon bond as the numeraire.

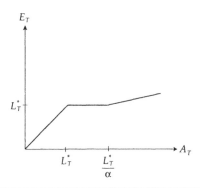

Figure 5-4   Policyholders' final payoffs

5.4 The required guaranteed interest rate and participation level

Policyholders do face the risk that their contract will not perform as initially planned. Shareholders can walk away if things go wrong. Policyholders are then paid on what is left. Consequently, they ask for a risk premium to compensate them for the risks they are carrying.

Policyholders have two ways to be rewarded for the risk of non-performance they face. For a given bonus δ, they will require a guaranteed rate r^* so that they do get a fair rate of return on their policy. Or, for a given r^*, they will make sure that the bonus level is such that the insurance policy offers an *ex-ante* fair rate of return. Viewed from the shareholders' side, the pricing of the insurance policy should be such that they are fairly compensated for owning the stock of the insurance company. This in turn means that the guaranteed rate and the bonus should be such that the initial cash outlay by shareholders is equal to the present value of their claim on future equity cashflows. But the present value of this claim is already known: it is given by expression (12). To put it even more simply, shareholders will not "subsidize" policyholders, nor will policyholders "subsidize" shareholders. Following Crouhy and Galai (1991), the equilibrium condition on both r^* and δ is thus given by:

$$(1-\alpha)\,A_0 = C_E\,(A_0\,,L_T^*) - \delta\alpha C_E\,(A_0\,,\frac{L_T^*}{\alpha}) \tag{18}$$

As a result, equation (18) gives either the guaranteed rate r^*, or the participation level δ, as the equilibrating variable. If δ is given, the guaranteed rate r^* remains to be determined, so that equation (18) is satisfied. If r^* is given, equation (18) yields the equilibrating value of the participation coefficient δ. It is worthwhile noting that, while r^* cannot be computed explicitly, an analytical expression for the participation coefficient δ can be derived:

$$\delta = \frac{C_E(A_0, L_T^*) - (1 - \alpha) A_0}{\alpha C_E(A_0, \frac{L_T^*}{\alpha})} \tag{19}$$

This model can thus be used to draw some pricing implications. In particular, the relationships linking the pricing parameters to the various inputs (volatility, leverage etc.) can be thoroughly examined.

5.4.1   The effect of total volatility on the level of the guaranteed interest rate

Figure 5-5 depicts the guaranteed rate r^* as a function of total volatility $\overline{\sigma}(t, T)$ for different participation levels δ.

The base case is that in which δ is equal to zero. Indeed, it corresponds to the situation analysed by Crouhy and Galai (1991). The interest rate r^* always increases when total volatility $\overline{\sigma}$ increases. This effect simply

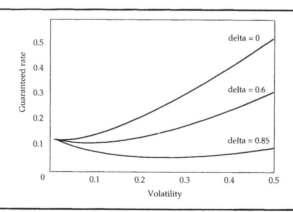

Figure 5-5   The guaranteed interest rate r^* as a function of total volatility $\overline{\sigma}$ ($\alpha = 0.9$, $T = 1$)

reflects an increasing risk premium required by policyholders for the growing risk they face.

The case of a non-zero δ is not as clear cut. It can, however, be shown that the curve linking r^* to $\overline{\sigma}$ is U-shaped. For low volatility levels, the guaranteed rate r^* is decreasing. For high volatility levels, r^* is increasing. Policyholders face a volatility dilemma. Indeed, they are both short a put to default and long a call to participate. On one hand, an increase in volatility makes the company more prone to default but, on the other, it has a positive effect on the policyholders' participation in the financial revenues of the insurance company. For low levels of volatility, this latter effect dominates. When the participation level δ increases, policyholders become more volatility prone.

5.4.2   The effect of total volatility on the level of the participation coefficient

Figure 5-6 depicts the relationship between δ and $\overline{\sigma}$ for various levels of the capital ratio α. The same pattern as before applies here. Policyholders are interested in volatility, as long as it is not too high. Again, this reflects the effect of their long call position.

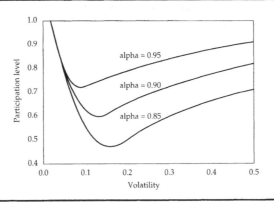

Figure 5-6   The participation coefficient δ as a function of total volatility $\overline{\sigma}$
($r^* = 0.12$, $T = 1$)

It is worthwhile noting that the equilibrating participation coefficient δ may well be below the French regulatory threshold of 85%, as shown by Figure 5-6. Forcing the company to apply a minimum 85% level may have two consequences: either the company reduces the riskiness of its assets (left shift), or it actually increases it (right shift). The second result is certainly not what is expected by regulators.

5.4.3   The impact of the leverage on the guaranteed rate

A greater financial leverage implies a higher financial risk, compensation for which has to be made. Figure 5-7 illustrates this effect.

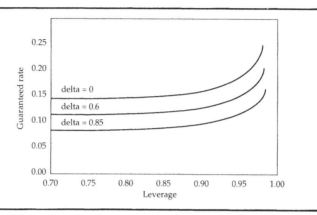

Figure 5-7   **The guaranteed interest rate r^* as a function of total volatility α**
($\bar{\sigma} = 0.1$, $T= 1$)

5.5 Regulatory implications

As mentioned by Klein (1993), "*the recent spate of insurer failures coming on the heels of the savings and loan disaster and problems in the banking industry has raised concerns about the adequacy of insurance regulation*". Many congressional investigations in the United States have indeed questioned whether the current regulatory system is able, effectively, both to supervise and to regulate insurance companies which are selling increasingly complex products. However, as stressed by Klein (1993), the current regulatory system is nevertheless in place and would certainly be costly to replace.

As far as life insurance companies are concerned, regulators usually envisage three main courses of action: first, they impose a minimum capital requirement. Second, they control asset compositions to prevent insurance companies from investing in risky ventures. Last, they introduce ceilings on the rates that can be guaranteed to policyholders. French regulators, as already mentioned, also impose a minimum level of participation of 85%.

In this section, we investigate the effects of such restrictions, whether they impact either on the asset side or the liability side. More specifically, we show that some of these regulations are, in fact, contradictory.

One of the most popular solvency regulations is the one governing the capital asset ratio. Even though the accurate amount of capital needed is still debated, the widespread belief is that a stringent capital asset ratio decreases the risk of bankruptcy. In our case, a stricter regulation on capital asset ratios entails a decrease in the participation coefficient δ. Policyholders carry less leverage risk and, as a consequence, lower their participation requirement, as is shown in Figure 5-8.

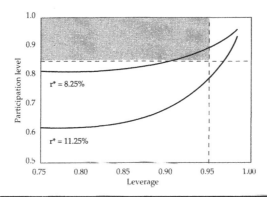

Figure 5-8   The participation coefficient δ as a function of the capital ration α ($\bar{\sigma} = 0.1$, $T = 1$)

However, imposing at the same time a minimum level for δ (such as 85%) may lead to inconsistencies. In Figure 5-8, the shaded area represents the feasibility area where both regulations, capital ratio (in France, α_{max} is roughly 95%) and participation level ($\delta_{min} = 85\%$) are effective. For an interest rate r^* equal to 11.25%, no equilibrating values can be found. Moreover, recent French regulation has introduced a ceiling on the interest rate r^*, which cannot exceed 75% of the Treasury bond rate average. Regulators claim that such a ceiling lessens the incentives of companies to invest in risky portfolios. Assume, in Figure 5-9, that a company wants to operate at the ceiling ($r^* = 75\% \times 15\% = 11.25\%$). Clearly, it cannot meet the minimum level of participation δ. The solution is then to lower the rate r^* to 8.25%. In that case, there are points in the second curve that lie within the shaded area, but this means that the ceiling regulation is useless. The constraint on the participation level δ is so stringent that the ceiling is thus redundant. In other words, the company is over-regulated.

The model enables us to understand, for instance, why "with profits" insurance policies are not widely sold in Germany, where the minimum level of participation δ is 95%. From Figure 5-8, we can see that such a level implies a very narrow shaded area, thus making it rather difficult for German insurance companies to operate.

Regulators also control the riskiness of assets and often impose asset restrictions. In our model, this translates into a constraint on the maximum level of volatility.

Assume that the company is operating at a rate r^*, which satisfies the ceiling constraint. Assume also that regulators impose a maximum volatility of 30%. One can see, from Figure 5-9, that less capitalized companies (δ close to 95%) have greater room for manoeuvre. Indeed, there are two asset structures ($\bar{\sigma} < 30\%$) for which the participation level δ is above its minimum. According to the well-known results of Galai and Masulis (1976), shareholders may then have an unexpected incentive to shift from the less risky structure to the riskier one. For well-capitalized companies, there is only one choice—which corresponds to a very low volatility level. At this low volatility level, they can enforce the minimum participation coefficient of 85%. Here again, given market forces, some regulations are either inconsistent or plainly redundant. Figures 5-8 and

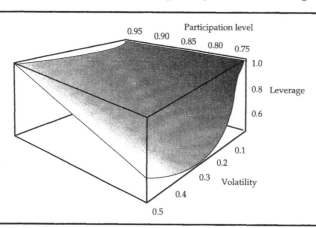

Figure 5-9   The relationship between the participation level δ, the capital ratio α and the total volatility $\bar{\sigma}$
($r^* = 0.1125$, $T = 1$)

5-9 also show that, for some values of the relevant parameters, the asset-structure constraint may be irrelevant. Indeed, assume that regulators impose a leverage constraint such that α has to be lower than 0.95 and that the asset restriction leads to a maximum volatility compatible with α equal to 0.95. It is then obvious that the floor constraint δ is strong enough to force insurance companies to migrate toward a low level of volatility (compatible with δ being at least equal to 0.85).

5.6   The interest-rate elasticity of life insurance liabilities

As indicated in the introduction to the chapter, this valuation model has some interesting implications for assessing the riskiness of a life insurance company. The assets and liabilities of a life insurance company are clearly interest-rate sensitive and so, to implement a sound asset-liability management approach, insurance managers need to evaluate accurately their exposure to these risks. Interest-rate elasticity and duration measures are now commonplace but, nevertheless, most of them are quite restrictive and only apply under a specific set of assumptions. Corporate default and bonus schemes are, for instance, rarely taken into account. This is unfortunate and produces biased estimates of the true elasticity of insurance liabilities. In that respect, our model is able to correct these pitfalls.

Let η_P, η_A and η_L denote, respectively, the interest-rate elasticity measure, as of time t, of the default-free zero-coupon bond $P(t, T)$, of the assets A_t, and of the life insurance liabilities L_t:

$$\eta_P(t, T) = -\frac{1}{P(t, T)} \cdot \frac{\partial P(t, T)}{\partial r_t} \tag{20}$$

$$\eta_A(t, T) = -\frac{1}{A_t} \cdot \frac{\partial A_t}{\partial r_t} \tag{21}$$

$$\eta_L(t, T) = -\frac{1}{L_t} \cdot \frac{\partial L_t}{\partial r_t} \tag{22}$$

Since the relationships between these variables and the short-term interest rate r_t are explicit, the interest-rate elasticity measures can be easily obtained by evaluating the partial derivatives of $P(t,T)$, A_t and L_t, with respect to r_t.

After some computations, we get:

$$\eta_P(t,T) = H(T-t) \qquad (23)$$

$$\eta_A(t,T) = -\frac{\rho\sigma_A}{\sigma} \qquad (24)$$

$$\eta_L(t,T) = \eta_P(t,T) - \frac{A_t}{L_t} \cdot [\eta_P(t,T) - \eta_A] \cdot [N(-d_1) + \delta\alpha N(d_3)] \quad (25)$$

From expression (25), several extreme cases can be recovered. The first deals with the situation where there is no bonus ($\delta = 0$) and the asset volatility σ_A is nil. Under these assumptions, the interest-rate elasticity of insurance liabilities reduces to:

$$\eta_L(t,T) = \eta_P(t,T) \qquad (26)$$

In other words, insurance liabilities have the same interest-rate elasticity as a default-free zero-coupon bond maturing at time T. This makes sense because insurance liabilities become just a default-free zero-coupon bond. In the second case, no bonus is attached to the insurance policy. Assets are, however, risky. As a result, expression (25) collapses to:

$$\eta_L(t,T) = \eta_P(t,T) - \frac{A_t}{L_t} \cdot [\eta_P(t,T) - \eta_A] \cdot N(-d_1) \qquad (27)$$

A careful inspection of expression (27) provides an illuminating insight into the more complex expression (25). Indeed, the right-hand side of expression (27) basically has two terms, the latter consisting of three factors. As mentioned above, the first term $\eta_P(t, T)$ corresponds to the interest-rate elasticity of a default-free zero-coupon bond. In the second term, the first factor A_t/L_t is a leverage ratio. The second factor $[\eta_P(t, T) - \eta_A]$ is the interest-rate elasticity gap between the default-free zero-coupon bond $\eta_P(t, T)$ and the insurance company's assets η_A. The third factor can be viewed as that which accounts for default risk.

Expression (25) is obviously more complex than expression (27). It reflects not only the above-mentioned effects, but also the influence of the bonus scheme. For policyholders, this bonus is equivalent to a long position on a call option, the interest-rate elasticity of which affects the total interest-rate elasticity of the insurance policy.

5.7   The duration of life insurance liabilities

When it comes to immunization or related techniques, practitioners use a duration tool (especially the Macaulay duration) more frequently than looking at interest-rate elasticity itself. Duration-matching methods are, for instance, quite popular. The accuracy of these methods, however, crucially depends on the correct measurement of duration. To provide results that are closer to current managerial practices, we now define the effective duration D_L of the insurance liabilities.

D_L is defined as the time-to-maturity of the default-free zero-coupon bond which exhibits the same interest-rate elasticity as the insurance liabilities. At time $t = 0$, D_L can be stated as the solution of the following equation:

$$\eta_L(0, T) = \eta_P(0, D_L) \tag{28}$$

where the left-hand side of the equation represents the interest-rate elasticity of life insurance liabilities, and the right-hand side the interest-rate elasticity of a default-free zero-coupon maturing in D_L periods.

In a Vasicek (1977) framework, expression (28) can be rewritten as of time $t = 0$ by:

$$D_L = \frac{\ln(1 - a\eta_L(0, T))}{a} \tag{29}$$

In this model, the traditional Macaulay duration of insurance liabilities is equal to the maturity of the life insurance policy. Indeed, there is no cash outflow between $t = 0$ and $t = T$.

To confirm the qualitative arguments put forward in Section 5.2, we now turn to a numerical implementation of our duration model. Figure 5-10 depicts the relationship between the initial duration of insurance liabilities and the maturity of the life insurance policy at time $t = 0$. It is based on the following basic parameter values: $\alpha = 0.8$, $\delta = 0.85$, $\sigma_A = 0.2$, $\sigma = 0.01$, $\rho = -0.2$, $a = 0.1$, $b = 0.1$ and $r_0 = 0.1$. A_0 is set to 1. In this numerical example, since the bonus level δ is fixed, the guaranteed rate r^* is computed according to the equilibrium condition (18) for each maturity. In Figure 5-10, the 45-degree line represents the locus of points where duration is exactly equal to maturity. In other words, it represents the Macaulay duration of the policy. A number of issues need to be addressed.

One can first observe that the effective duration of insurance liabilities is generally smaller than the maturity, i.e. the Macaulay duration. Insurance liabilities are composed of three terms. The short position in the default put reduces the duration of insurance liabilities, so does the

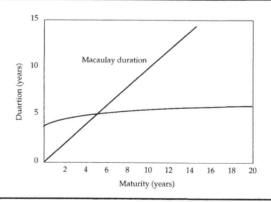

Figure 5-10   Liabilities duration as a function of time-to-maturity

long position in the bonus call option. Indeed, the call is an increasing function of the interest rate. For instance, life insurance liabilities with a maturity of 20 years have an effective duration of 6.23 years. However, this result does not carry over to short-term insurance liabilities. In this example, for a maturity of less than 5 years the effective duration is greater than the Macaulay duration. This result may seem to be quite counterintuitive. The lengthening of the effective duration finds its main roots in the bonus scheme and the interest-rate elasticity gap between the default-free zero-coupon bond and the insurance company's assets as can be seen in expression (25). In the case of a negative correlation[6] (which we have here) and short maturities, the gap is negative: asset duration[7] is higher than maturity. The risk of life insurance liabilities is a more complex issue than conventional wisdom might suggest. As we noted in Section 5.2, life insurers frequently insist upon the long maturity (i.e. duration) of their liabilities. The message conveyed by our contingent-claim approach is somewhat different and boils down to: "short means long, long means short".[8]

A last point concerning Figure 5-10 deserves some explanation. When the maturity of the life insurance liability is zero, it appears that the effective duration is not nil (in Figure 5-10, it is roughly equal to three). Such a result is strongly at odds with what intuition would suggest. However, a careful investigation of expression (25) provides an important clue. The effective duration of insurance liabilities is driven by the duration of assets through the bonus mechanism. When the bonus is nil, intuition is restored: effective duration is equal to zero because, at time $t = 0$:

$$\begin{cases} \lim_{T \to 0} \overline{\sigma}(0, T)\sqrt{T} = 0 \\ \lim_{T \to 0} L_T^* = L_0 \\ \lim_{T \to 0} d_1 = + \infty \end{cases} \quad \text{which imply} \quad \lim_{T \to 0} \eta_L(0, T) = 0 \quad (30)$$

Again, the message conveyed by our model is clear: "very short means quite long!"

---

[6] This assumption is obviously a reasonable one.

[7] Which does not depend on the maturity of the insurance policy.

[8] Under our set of assumptions.

Figure 5-10 yields interesting results. One could, however, argue that it does not clearly disentangle the respective effects of the shareholders' option to default and the bonus scheme. To cope with this, some more numerical simulations are implemented. More specifically, in Figure 5-11, a life insurance policy with a maturity of 10 years is considered. In this graph, the effective initial duration D_L of the life insurance liabilities is related to the insurance company leverage ratio α at time $t = 0$. The parameters are set with the same values as in Figure 5-10. For low leverage ratios, the effect of the put to default is significantly neutralized. The bulk of the impact on the effective duration of the insurance liability stream stems primarily from the bonus scheme. Indeed, in the corner case, where the leverage ratio is close to zero, the effective duration of the insurance policy with a typical bonus of 85% is roughly 60% of that of a policy with no bonus at all.

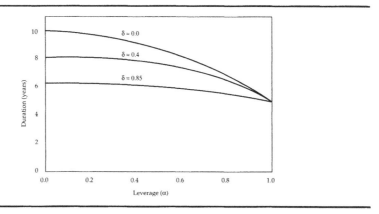

Figure 5-11   Liabilities duration as a function of leverage

5.8 Why does equity behave like a short straddle?

A relevant objective of any asset-liability management policy in a life insurance company is to ensure that equity is not sensitive to unexpected shifts in interest rates. Indeed, shareholders do not need a cumbersome vehicle such as a life insurance company to speculate on the future course of interest rates, since they can do it themselves—and more efficiently—by buying/selling bonds or interest-rate futures contracts.

In what follows we look at the implications of our previous results for the asset-liability posture of the life insurance company. The market value of equity is obviously equal to the difference between the market value of assets and the market value of liabilities. As such, its effective duration is directly affected by both the duration of assets, the duration of liabilities and the leverage effect. More specifically, at time t, we know that $A_t = E_t + L_t$. If η_A, η_E and η_L denote, respectively, the interest-rate elasticity of assets, equity and insurance liabilities, we have:

$$\eta_A(t,T) = \frac{E_t}{A_t}\cdot\eta_E(t,T) + \frac{L_t}{A_t}\cdot\eta_L(t,T) \tag{31}$$

Equation (31) is useful for extrapolating η_E:

$$\eta_E(t,T) = \eta_P(t,T) - \frac{A_t}{E_t}\cdot[\eta_P(t,T)-\eta_A]\cdot[N(d_1)-\delta\alpha N(d_3)] \tag{32}$$

To investigate how changes in interest rates affect the market value E_t of the equity, we take as a starting point for the analysis the closed-form solution in equation (12). A non-expected change in the short-term interest rate r_t affects E_t through the riskless zero-coupon bond $P(t, T)$ and through the asset value A_t. However, equations (4) for $P(t,T)$ and (5) for A_t provide the explicit relationships between these variables and r_t.

If r_t denotes the initial short-term interest rate at time t, and $\hat{r}_t$ represents its new value after an instantaneous non-expected change, then it is possible to calculate, from equations (4) and (5), the new values of both, $\hat{P}(t,T,\hat{r}_t)$ and $\hat{A}_t(\hat{r}_t)$:

$$\hat{P}(t,T,\hat{r}_t) = G(T-t)\cdot\exp(-H(T-t)\hat{r}_t) \tag{33}$$

$$\hat{A}_t(\hat{r}_t) = A_t\cdot\exp(-\eta_A(\hat{r}_t-r_t)) \tag{34}$$

Figure 5-12 portrays the behaviour of equity value as a function of the level of the interest rate. To draw such a picture, the following parameter values are used: $T = 10, \alpha = 0.8, \delta = 0.85, \sigma_A = 0.2, \sigma = 0.01, a = 0.1, b = 0.1, r_0 =$

0.1 and $A_0 = 1$. The correlation coefficient ρ is set such that the equity interest-rate elasticity η_E is equal to zero for the initial interest rate r_0. The guaranteed interest rate r^* is equal to the optimal rate, as defined by the equilibrium condition (18) corresponding to these correlation coefficient and interest-rate parameters. With our set of parameters, we obtain $\rho = -0.12894$ and $r^* = 0.07735$.

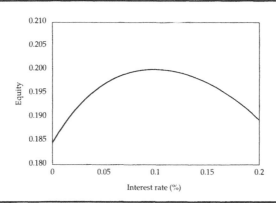

Figure 5-12   Equity as a function of interest rate

The striking feature of Figure 5-12 is that equity behaves like a short straddle. In option markets, a short straddle is achieved by simultaneously selling a put and a call on the same underlying asset. The rationale for choosing such a profile is to gain from small movements in the price of the underlying asset, whatever the direction. Providing these price changes remain small, neither the call nor put will be exercised by the long side, while the short side of the straddle ensures that the seller retains the option premiums. In case of large movements, however, this short straddle position can clearly prove risky, as the call or put is more likely to be exercised and the loss from the exercise could exceed the gain from the premiums.

From Figure 5-12 and its set of parameters, one can observe that the duration of equity is nil at a 10% interest rate. If interest rates go below that level, the slope becomes positive: when interest rates decrease, the value of equity goes down. Beyond that level, the slope is negative: when rates increase, the value of equity decreases. The fact that the equity of a life insurance company may resemble a short straddle is not new, having already been described in 1989 by Babbel and Stricker. However, their framework is quite different and their short straddling equity is a direct result of their choices for assets and liabilities. In their model, insureds hold a surrender option, namely the equivalent of an American put option on a zero-coupon bond. On the asset side, the company, in its quest for extra yields, is assumed to invest in callable bonds. By buying such bonds, the insurance company implicitly sells an American call bond option to the issuer. The short straddle outcome is then quite straightforward: the insurance company ends up selling options not only on the liability side, but also on the asset side. In our setting, this explanation is not valid. For instance, no option is assumed to be sold on the asset side and no surrender option is considered. The only options at work are the put to default and the bonus call option—both being on the liability side. The concavity of equity[9] is the by-product of the interest rate risk exposure of assets and liabilities and the leverage effect. As a result, even in a very simple framework, the insurance company may turn out to be betting its equity on interest rates. To clarify why a short straddle is obtained, it may be useful to disentangle the various effects at play on both the asset side and the liability side.

Figure 5-13 depicts these various effects by relating the relative change in assets, liabilities and equity values to the level of the interest rate at time $t = 0$. The behaviour of the life insurance liabilities with respect to the interest rate is computed in the same way as equity in Figure 5-12. Given the choice of (reasonable) parameters, liabilities and assets are shown to exhibit a classical convex behaviour. The convexity effect is, however, stronger on the liability side than on the asset side. When interest rates go down, assets tend to go up because of the negative correlation and the total effect on the bonus call option is a positive one. Liabilities increase more than they would in the absence of a bonus. When interest rates go up, assets tend to decrease and the dominant effect is that of the put to default which goes deeper in-the-money. Liabilities lose more value than they would if no default were possible. As a result, liabilities turn out to be more convex than assets. The consequence for equity is immediate: it exhibits a negative convexity. In Figure 5-13, equity is immune from interest-rate risk at a 10% interest rate. However, any change from that level entails a diminution of shareholder value.

---

[9] A "negative gamma" to use option pricing terminology.

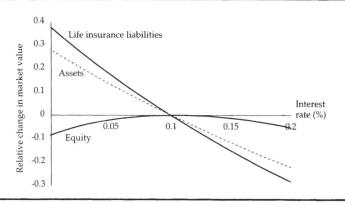

Figure 5-13   The relative impact of changes in interest rates

To avoid such a prospect—that is, speculating on interest rates on behalf of shareholders—assets must be allocated such that their duration results in a zero-duration for equity. To show that this is possible, equity duration is related to asset duration in Figure 5-14. Because the interest-rate elasticity of assets is given by $\eta_A = -\rho\sigma_A/\sigma$, asset allocation policies can be mimicked by tuning the correlation coefficient for a given level of asset volatility. Indeed, a lower coefficient means that the asset portfolio is more heavily invested in bonds. On the contrary, a higher coefficient implies that the portfolio is geared toward equity investment. In Figure 5-13, an asset duration of 2.58 years, namely a correlation coefficient ρ equal to –0.12894, yields a zero equity duration. A greater asset duration would imply a company betting on a decrease in interest rates.

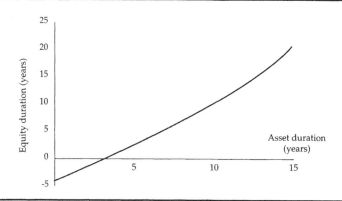

Figure 5-14   Equity duration as a function of asset duration

A last implication of our results is that derivatives, like options or structured products, are certainly good candidates for fine-tuning equity immunization strategies. Indeed, to compensate negative convexity effects, buying options[10] on the asset side is a strategy that deserves careful consideration.

5.9   Conclusion

Recently, life insurance companies have been forced to redesign their product lines, the most obvious consequence of which has been a shift toward interest-rate sensitive policies. Thus, life insurance companies have, in turn, become more sensitive to interest-rate movements than they were in the past. This trend occurs at a time when an unprecedented tide of financial insolvency has raised growing concerns among politicians, claimholders, and regulators.

By relying on a contingent-claims valuation framework, the model presented in this chapter attempts to capture the various risks that life insurance carries, while neutralizing some of the pitfalls commonly encountered in the industry. Asset risk, interest-rate risk, default risk, and leverage risk have all been considered and their respective effects on the insurance company—and its solvency—have been assessed. More specifically, a competitive market assumption, combined with an option pricing framework, shows how assets and liabilities are intertwined. We have also considered the implications of a specific asset structure and a particular leverage ratio, together with the level of default-free interest rates required for the contractual features of "with profits" policies. Furthermore, we have also delved into some relevant aspects of regulation.

Since the model accounts for stochastic interest rates, default risk and bonus schemes, it produces more accurate interest-rate elasticity and duration measures. The effective duration of life insurance liabilities has been shown to be significantly different from the traditional Macaulay duration measure. For reasonable sets of parameters, equity resembles a short straddle, even though we did not rely on the traditional

---

[10] *In other words, buying positive convexity.*

explanations to achieve such a result. Immunization implications have also been considered.

The framework presented here is fairly general. However, one of the most obvious progenies of the model is the introduction of so-called "embedded options". Indeed, most life insurance policies now contain various option variations, such as policy loan options and early lapsation options. For instance, when insureds are allowed to drop out early while being guaranteed a fixed rate, their position is equivalent to a long position on a (zero-coupon) bond put option. In such a case, it is to be expected that, *ceteris paribus*, the participation level δ should be lower. However, imposing a floor on δ may bring about some unexpected consequences and it could imply that embedded options are mispriced. Since embedded options amount to selling options to policyholders, introducing them would actually amplify the effect we have outlined, as liabilities would be even more sensitive to increases in interest rates. This is precisely what our *ALM Survival Toolkit*, in the Appendix to this book, is all about.

References

Babbel, D. and Stricker, R., *Asset/Liability Management for Insurers, Insurance Perspectives*, Goldman Sachs (1989)

Beaver, W., Data, S., and Wolson, M., "The Role of Market Value Accounting in the Regulations of Insured Depository Institutions", Working Paper, Stanford University (1990)

Bernard, V.L., Merton, R.C., and Palepu, K.G., "Mark-to-market Accounting for US Banks and Thrifts: Lessons from the Danish Experience", Working Paper 93-034, Harvard Business School (1993)

Black, F. and Scholes, M., "The Pricing of Options and Corporate Liabilities", *Journal of Political Economy*, 84 (1973), 637–659

Brennan, M.J., "Aspects of Insurance, Intermediation and Finance", *Geneva Papers on Risk and Insurance Theory*, 18(1) (1993), 7–30

Briys, E. and de Varenne, F., "Life Insurance in a Contingent Claims Framework: Pricing and Regulatory Implications", *The Geneva Papers on Risk and Insurance Theory*, vol. 19, n°1 (June 1994), 53–72

Briys, E. and de Varenne, F., "On the Risk of Insurance Liabilities: Debunking some Common Pitfalls", *Journal of Risk and Insurance*, vol. 64, no. 4 (1997), 673–694

Crouhy, M. and Galai, D., "A Contingent Claim Analysis of a Regulated Depository Institution", *Journal of Banking and Finance*, 15 (1991), 73–90

Cummins, J.D., "Risk-based Premiums for Insurance Guaranty Funds", *Journal of Finance*, 43 (1988), 823–839

Cummins, J.D., Harrington, S., and Niehaus, G., "Risk-based Capital Requirements for Property-Liability Insurers: An Analysis of Conceptual and Measurement Issues", paper presented at the Conference on the Dynamics of the Insurance Industry, New York University Salomon Center, May 20–21 (1993)

D'Arcy, S. and Doherty, N.A., *The Financial Theory of Pricing Property-Liability Insurance Contracts*, Huebner Foundation Monograph 15, Wharton School, University of Pennsylvania (1988)

Galai, D. and Masulis, R., "The Option Pricing Model and the Risk Factor of Stock", *Journal of Financial Economics*, 3 (1976), 53–81

Ingersoll, J.E. Jr., *Theory of Financial Decision Making*, Rownam & Littlefield (1987)

Klein, R.W., "Solvency Monitoring of Insurance Companies: Regulators" Role and Future Direction", paper presented at the Conference on the Dynamics of the Insurance Industry, New York University Salomon Center, May 20–21 (1993)

Merton, R.C., "Theory of Rational Option Pricing", *Bell Journal of Economics and Management Science*, 4 (1973), 141–183

Merton, R.C., "An Analytic Derivation of the Cost of Deposit Insurance and Loan Guarantees", *Journal of Banking and Finance*, 1 (1977), 3–11

Merton, R.C., "On the Cost of Deposit Insurance when there are Surveillance Costs", *Journal of Business* 51 (1978), 439–452

Merton, R.C., "On the Application of the Continuous-Time Theory of Finance to Financial Intermediation and Insurance", *Geneva Papers on Risk and Insurance*, 14 (52) (1989), 225–261

Merton, R.C., *Continuous Time Finance*, Basil Blackwell, Cambridge (1990)

Vasicek, O., "An Equilibrium Characterization, of the Term Structure", *Journal of Financial Economics*, 7 (1977), 117–161

White, L.J., *The S&L Debacle*, Oxford University Press (1991)

Wright, K.M., "The Structure Conduct and Regulation of the Life Insurance Industry", in R.W. Kopcke and R.E. Randall (Eds), *The Financial Condition and Regulation of Insurance Companies*, Federal Reserve Bank of Boston (1991)

Chapter 6

A Functional Approach to the Insurance Industry

6.1 Introduction

We all use financial services. We may have already used them, or we may use them in the future but, like death and tax, they are inescapable. When we do use them, we acquire a certain classification, whether it be as a policyholder, a borrower or a saver. However, despite the generic term "financial services", most people can see a clear distinction between, say, the role of a policyholder and bank customer. Indeed, the mere existence of banks and insurance companies as separate entities is taken for granted and their respective products and services are not perceived in the same way. For instance, many consumers consider the payment of a property-casualty insurance premium to be a decision that is quite divorced from that of buying a mortgage. Of course, such distinctions are not genetic in origin. We have been programmed to think that way and this behaviour has been reinforced by numerous regulatory, fiscal and institutional factors.

That said, the recent changes—or, more accurately, upheavals—that have shaken the world of financial markets and services necessitate a drastic revision of our perception and understanding of the role of financial institutions. The markets have developed an ever-expanding range of instruments and techniques that have boosted their importance within our economies. For example, in the United States, commercial banks have been driven out of their traditional mortgage market through the intensive use of securitization techniques. As a result, new asset classes have been created and capital markets are displaying a relish for the risks that, until now, have always been the domain of insurance and reinsurance companies. This seemingly insatiable appetite clearly raises many challenging questions, not to say concerns, about the future of financial intermediaries.

Indeed, many observers are seriously questioning the benefits of this massive expansion of what they term the "virtual economy". For instance, they claim that the current pace of financial innovation may eventually lead to an increase in systemic risk. Specifically, they see the proliferation of derivatives as potentially disruptive to the real economy. We challenge this view. Indeed, we believe that there is a specific derivatives viewpoint. Derivatives are not merely financial instruments traded on organized markets or over-the-counter (OTC), they represent something far greater. They deliver a very powerful framework through which practitioners can decipher current and future market trends for financial institutions. This chapter focuses primarily on insurance companies. Insurance policies and derivative "put" options (i.e. options which give the holder the right to sell at a given price) are intimately related and this next-of-kin relationship carries far-reaching implications, which we shall discuss in depth.

Our examination will be broadly chronological. In the first section, we revisit history as we follow a Genoa merchant of the Middle Ages, whose entrepreneurial venture required some suprisingly sophisticated risk transfer techniques. The lessons that one can draw from this historical experience are particularly useful. While the first section describes the traditional approach to financial intermediaries, with a strong emphasis on insurance companies, the second section seeks to challenge this rather old-fashioned view and examines new angles to deepen our under-standing of the future of insurance (and reinsurance) companies. The third section looks at the far-reaching implications of this "brave new world" both for insurance companies in particular and financial intermediaries in general. The fourth and final section examines some of the wider implications.

6.2 The Genoa merchant

The quirks of Mother Nature have always posed a threat to mankind. In ancient times, peasants—whose sole means of subsistence came from working the land—would seek to ward off these natural perils by visiting their simple pantheons and enlisting the assistance of benevolent saints and gods. In Burgundy, a French province famous for its magnificent wines, wine growers would pray to Saint Medard and Sainte Barbe for clement weather. Indeed, Saint Medard was venerated on the grounds of his ability to make rain, while Sainte Barbe's ability to chase away lightning remains legendary. However, this celestial form of coverage was usually supplemented with some down-to-earth form of hedging. For instance, sea navigators would not only pray to Saint Guenole, but would also prudently arrange some contracts to mitigate their exposure to sea perils.

Indeed, marine navigation has always been a hazardous venture and this was one of the primary risks faced by medieval businessmen. As Jean Favier (1987) writes, *"Travel by sea was definitely the foremost trade risk."* The dangers were numerous, to say the least: tempests could destroy a merchant's efforts and capital in one blow; entire vessels, along with their precious cargoes, could be swallowed by surging currents. Meanwhile, navigators had to rely solely on astral signposts, and were even denied these when the weather turned; captains and crewmates could only count on their experience and courage. Even when the weather was calm, there was always the ever-present danger from greedy buccaneers and corsairs which preyed on merchant shipping, stealing cargo and selling crew members into slavery (if they were lucky!). This concentration of risks upon a single focus, the ship, made sea travel a life-threatening business and should, in itself, have led to a slowdown in the growth of trade.

Yet marine trade continued to grow and to link ever more remote geographical points as merchants began to use larger vessels capable of sailing farther from the safety of coastlines. Escorts were offered to discourage attack but, while this was safer, it also came at a price and thus raised the cost of trade. In Venice, for example, merchants had a clear choice: they could either use private ships without escort and take their chances or, for an additional fee, they could sail under the protection of official vessels. The cost rendered the choice a difficult one. There was no doubt that armed fleets discouraged the boldest of pirates, but their cost was prohibitive and substantially eroded profits. It was far cheaper to sail without protection, provided the ship actually reached its destination! Shipowners in Marseilles dealt with this dilemma by inventing the system of the crown to spread the risk over several merchants. In 1387, 14 merchants from Marseilles formed a crown to operate a ship at a total cost of 2,000 florins, with every participant contributing from 30 to 200 florins. While this reduced individual jeopardy, the risk was not entirely transferred and some improvements were necessary.

According to Jean Favier (1987), a Genoa merchant named Benedetto Zaccaria had to ship 30 tons of alum in 1298 from Aigues-Mortes to Bruges, where he had located a buyer. Zaccaria was aware of the contingencies and, with the help of two Genoa financiers, Baliano Grilli and Enrico Suppa, he struck a contract which was specifically designed to shift the risk away from his merchant shipping business. This is how it worked: Zaccaria sold the alum to Suppa and Grilli on the spot at an agreed price. The alum was then loaded on a vessel that would head for Bruges. Provided the vessel reached Bruges safely, Zaccaria was committed to repurchase the alum from Suppa and Grilli, after which he would then sell it to his local client. Naturally, the repurchase price was much higher than the price of the initial spot transaction. However, if things went wrong due, say, to a storm, and the alum went lost during the voyage, Zaccaria would not owe a thing to Suppa and Grilli. In other words, Suppa and Grilli granted Zaccaria an option to default on the repurchase transaction. A modern economist would simply say that the three Genoa businessmen had come up with a non-linear risk sharing rule. Viewed from Zaccaria's standpoint, the risk sharing rule is convex: he was long (i.e. owned) an option to default. Moreover, the transaction offered the considerable advantage of being accepted by such scholars as Saint Thomas, who condemned the very notion of interest rates. The transaction between Zaccaria, Suppa and Grilli was subtle, since it involved only sales and repurchase operations, and so the theological concept of *damnum emergens* prevailed: there was a physical risk, for which it was deemed legitimate to compensate. Thus, two problems were solved simultaneously by a single structure. By acquiring the option, Zaccaria had not abandoned his role as a merchant. On the contrary, the transfer of an exogenous risk to people who felt capable of underwriting it enabled him to focus better on his business. The physical and ecclesiastical bogies were duly dealt with. Suppa and Grilli negotiated an attractive repurchase price, and underwrote Zaccaria's physical marine risk without incurring the wrath of ecclesiasts.

But can we tell more about Suppa and Grilli? Were they insurers, bankers or derivative traders? Did Zaccaria subscribe to an insurance policy? Did he strike an investment banking deal, or purely a capital market transaction? Bankers will obviously claim the paternity of the deal since, after all, Zaccaria had paid no up-front premium to Suppa and Grilli. Insurers would dismiss this as nonsense, claiming that Suppa and Grilli had acted as an insurance company because they agreed to underwrite the entire burden of the risk. In other words, Zaccaria signed an insurance contract with Suppa and Grilli. Interestingly enough, Zaccaria had no intention of bracketing himself either as an insured party or as a bank client. What mattered to him was to be relieved from a risk that was beyond his expertise and control.

Yet this answer does not satisfy either insurers or bankers. Twenty-first century insurers dislike being compared to bankers and the converse is probably also true. In other words, if Suppa and Grilli were insurers, they could not also be bankers, and vice versa. That said, modern consumers of financial services draw a similar line of distinction between banks and insurance companies.

This is hardly surprising. Banks and insurance companies are subject to different regulations and are governed by different supervisory authorities. Both have their own industry organizations. For consumers, the regulations covering bank loans differ from those of insurance contracts. If they were living in the twenty-first century, Enrico Suppa and Baliano Grilli would have to opt for a precise "institutional status", while Benedetto Zaccaria would have had to choose whether to be a bank client or a policyholder.

6.3 Banking and insurance: the traditional approach

Obviously, many factors have contributed to this differentiation between banks and insurance companies. For example, insurers have energetically pleaded their case and advocated the unique nature of their business. This distinction is traditionally fuelled by three key arguments:

- the so-called "inversion" of the insurance production cycle;
- liability risk-taking; and
- the duration of liabilities.

The first argument, which occurs quite frequently in major actuarial sciences and insurance management textbooks, states that the insurance production cycle is unique. The sale price of insurance (the premium) must be determined before its true cost price (its cost in the event of a claims) is known. However, an insurance company does not know whether or not a loss will occur and, furthermore, cannot quantify the extent of any potential loss. At best, it must rely upon the law of large numbers by grouping a large cohort of policyholders within the same insurance portfolio. Insurance pricing therefore requires a very special expertise and that is the job of the "rocket scientists" of insurance that go by the name of *actuaries*.

According to the second argument, an insurance company selling an insurance contract accepts a contingent commitment that adds to its liabilities. Conversely, a banker granting a real estate or commercial loan holds a claim that is added to its assets. The insurance company is a debtor to its client. Writing an insurance contract is tantamount to issuing a promise.

The third argument focuses on the length of commitments accepted by insurance companies, especially life insurance companies. Annuity payments span a significant length of time and the servicing period can be far longer than expected due to the risk of longevity.

These arguments tend to suggest that matters have changed a great deal since the thirteenth century. Indeed, at first sight, it may seem that insurance companies have become a unique breed, a world apart from banks. However, this distinction is erroneous, since banking and insurance are not really dissimilar activities. Benedetto Zaccaria knew that a long time ago!

The first argument can be negated by two simple examples. Options markets quote call and put prices—even though option buyers and sellers do not know in advance whether or not their options will be exercised. In the case of mortgages, banks grant prepayment options and must therefore price in a provision that may, or may not, be used (exercised) by the client. Suppa and Grilli were in the same situation. They could not foretell whether Zaccaria would call on them to bail him out of a disaster, or whether he would complete his voyage safely. In case of a loss at sea, or an act of piracy, Zaccaria would exercise his right to default. In other words, although insurers do not actually use the word *option*, selling an insurance contract is nevertheless tantamount to selling an option contract! The policyholder pays a premium to the insurer for the right to transfer his or her loss to the insurance company. It is clear, therefore, that an insurance contract and an option functionally provide the same service. The holder of a put option has the guarantee that the value of the asset at risk is protected by the put. Automobile insurance is a good example: when a loss exceeds the insurance deductible (the premium), a policyholder will exercise his or her right to indemnification. The difference between the value of the loss and the deductible will thus be the perceived net receipt. By contrast, if the loss is less than the deductible, there will be no net receipt and the loss will therefore be effectively paid for by the policyholder. The boundaries between insurance and derivatives are quite blurred. The recent development of the so-called *catastrophe bond* offers another good example, as shown in Chapter 2. These bonds are characterized by the fact that their coupons and/or their principal are exposed to the occurrence of natural catastrophes. Their potential yield is usually high in order to compensate the lender for the possible loss of the coupons and/or principal to which he is entitled. In other words, the lender acts as if he were an insurance company by insuring the borrower against damages caused by the occurrence of natural catastrophes. In the case of a claim, the borrower pays back nothing and can therefore use the funds that are not reimbursed to cover his losses. For example, Winterthur, the Swiss insurance company, recently floated a bond in order to hedge itself against hail risk, since heavy hailstones can result in significant vehicle body damage. Traditionally, insurance companies cede part of their risks to reinsurance companies. However, in this case, Winterthur has chosen an alternative institutional arrangement through the transfer of the hailstone risk to the financial market by means of an instrument that bears a strong resemblance to the solution used several centuries ago by the Genoa merchant Benedetto Zaccaria!

The second argument is also quite easy to quash. Bank deposits can be viewed as providing liquidity insurance. A deposit-holder knows that, in the case of unexpected liquidity needs, he can cash-in his deposit, either totally or in part. The analogy with insurance in this case is even stronger: due to the law of large numbers, not everyone is expected to run and withdraw deposits at the same instant, and it is this same notion of risk mutualization lies precisely at the heart of the insurance industry. To support this counter-argument further, we can point to the existence of indexed CDs (Certificates of Deposit). Banks offer CDs, the return of which comprises a fixed component plus a variable component which is pegged to a specific index. By issuing such deposits, banks are indeed taking risks, since they guarantee a floor and also provide a potential bonus.

The third argument can also be countered effectively. Life insurance companies frequently demand a long maturity for their liabilities. This long-term view stems from the actuarial dimension of insurance liabilities, a typical example being the life annuity that is paid until death, which may occur very late on. Until recently, as stressed by Wright (1991), *"portfolio philosophy in the life insurance business was centered on the matching of assets and liabilities... The traditional practices of buying long-term bonds and mortgages and holding them to maturity were based on the long duration of liabilities."* Wright hastens to add that, today *"a rethinking of the duration of these (insurance) products is essential"*. This rethinking is not only urged by the redesign of life insurance policies themselves, but also by the pressure of competition. Insurance agents bring considerable pressure on companies' headquarters to set initial rates high enough to match competition and to keep them high in the future, even though interest rates might have fallen. These interwoven effects challenge the long-term view of insurance liabilities. The duration—in other words, the interest-rate risk exposure of insurance liabilities—is not merely a matter of mortality table analysis and proper discounting, it is also significantly affected by the "geometry" of the contractual liability cashflows. Since insurance liabilities are not traded, and as accounting practices tend to distort the cashflow picture, this last point is often not clearly understood. Many insurance companies continue to manage their liabilities using a long-term horizon, when they should generally be aiming at a much shorter timeframe.

All this suggests that the traditional analysis of insurance companies must be revised. There is much to be learned from the alleged "convergence" between insurance markets and financial markets. Indeed, there is little to differentiate the principles involved in the insurance and derivative sectors, for an insurance contract fulfils the same function as a put option. In a nutshell, traditional insurance underwriting and derivatives writing are two sides of the same coin.

6.4 The virtual economy and the need for functional analysis

The Genoa merchant, Zaccaria, wanted to protect his business against seagoing hazards and the threats of piracy. He was primarily interested in transferring his risk to outside players and, in 1298, he chose a hybrid solution that could have been engineered by an insurer, a speculator or a banker. The key question is therefore not whether there is a genetic difference between insurance companies and banks, but rather whether those in the position of Zaccaria can focus on their core talents without the fear of adversity from uncontrollable events. Fortunately, a vast array of solutions is available through institutional arrangements on offer from banks, insurance companies, financial markets and others. This makes it possible to select the optimum institution for the function that needs to be fulfilled and it is rather fortunate that modern capital markets in the *virtual economy* provide effective tools which address an ever-increasing array of risks faced by those operating in the *real economy*. In other words, there is no "black hole" between the real and virtual economies. The virtual economy is of fundamental importance since it addresses the problems of opacity and incompleteness which exist in the real economy. It empowers real market players by enabling them to retain only those risks that are fundamentally tied to their talents. Furthermore, by lifting the veil and reducing opacity, the virtual economy enhances the operation of the real economy. Remember that the transport and sale of alum was part of Zaccaria's principal business. Once freed from the dangers of the sea, he still had to ensure that his business was both attractive to customers and financially viable. To this end, he could employ his real-world acumen. The same applies to banks and insurance companies. To maintain market share, they have to show their clients that the services and products they provide are both useful and legitimate. However, this is not always easy to prove, as demonstrated in the United States, for example, where commercial banks have gradually been driven out of the mortgage market. Much of their business has been swallowed up by financial market operators and specialist investment banks and, today, mortgages are tradable on a buoyant mortgage-backed securities market. In essence, then, the financing of mortgages has broken free from its traditional master and has become a free agent.

The virtual economy also holds significant opportunities for anyone with genuine expertise. A few years ago, it was hard to imagine that anyone could diversify his or her expertise without running the risk of losing it. The example of fund managers is a very telling one. Every day, these managers engage in a ceaseless quest for that Holy Grail of finance: *maximum yield at minimum risk*! For many years, Switzerland enjoyed a privileged position in the private banking market but, today, the market has ceased to be a uniquely Swiss domain. New competition has emerged and this is not solely attributable to the newly-discovered fragility in the traditional virtue of Swiss confidentiality. There is more to it than that. For instance, any US fund manager who specializes in US corporate bonds and swaps the performance of an American corporate bond index against a Swiss equity index becomes a formidable competitor for the Swiss private banker since, by using such a swap, the US manager can turn a US corporate bond portfolio into a Swiss equity portfolio. Indeed, the following sequence of events, albeit invented, could serve as a useful example of the opportunities available in the virtual economy. A client wants a highly talented corporate bond manager to invest SFr100m in the Swiss equity market. The manager could decline the business by virtue of the fact that he is not an equity manager, but he cleverly devises a work-round. He invests the sum in one of his managed corporate bond portfolios and simultaneously swaps the performance of a US corporate bond index against the performance of the Swiss equity index. Thanks to this exchange, the real bond portfolio has become a virtual Swiss equity portfolio. Although its physical structure has not changed, its cashflows walk and talk like Swiss equity cashflows. Let us suppose, in this example, that the US corporate bond index exhibits an 11% return, while the Swiss equity index shows a 12% return. As a direct result of his genuine expertise, the bond manager has outperformed the US corporate bond index by 1% (after deducting his fees). But what does this mean for the Swiss client? He receives a profit equal to 12% + (13% − 11%), i.e. 14%! Although the US corporate bond manager knows nothing about equity—and even less about the Swiss market—the magic of the swap enables him to export his know-how without leaving home!

Competition continues to mushroom, and it can sprout from anywhere, even from within (a Brazilian manager specializing in Brazilian equity can face a threat that comes from Brazil itself!). Banks, insurance companies and financial intermediaries are therefore now facing significant challenges and, to survive and prosper, they must face up to the vexed question of how to identify their value-added contribution and to discover how can it be exported and improved. According to an old saying, someone who is good at everything is good at nothing. But to be good at anything, one has to be good at something. In a sense, modern finance resembles Proteus, the Greek god of the sea, who could change form at will.

Insurance companies have not been spared the effects of the emerging virtual economy. In the United States, catastrophe and weather-related risks are now traded both on organized and over-the-counter markets. Of course, the implications of these changes are far-reaching and lead to some fascinating issues, such as the convergence between insurance pricing and financial pricing. This, in itself, will trigger major changes in the insurance industry. For example, in the specific area of credit insurance and credit derivatives, the price discrepancies between the two are huge and, even after factoring contractual provision differences into the equation, it is difficult to reconcile the two methods of pricing. That said, the interim convergence phase nevertheless provides some rather profitable arbitrage opportunities.

6.5 Should insurance companies be afraid of the big bad wolf?

Thanks to virtual derivatives engineering, all market players, whoever and wherever they may be, have the opportunity to express their talent. Of course, this freedom naturally leads to an ever-increasing variety of product and, if there is one tyrannical aspect of virtual derivatives finance, this is where it lies. Due to the blossoming range of modern financial instruments, the virtual economy is constantly putting the real economy to test. Modern finance is particularly demanding and challenging and it is engaged in a ceaseless process of renewal, where old formulae die out and make way for new solutions. At first sight, this powerful drive may appear to be the direct result of the virtual market "doing its own thing", but in fact it owes its strength to the magnitude of the daily problems faced by players in the real economy. Eight centuries after the event, there seems nothing unusual about Benedetto Zaccaria's indifference as to whether Enrico Suppa and Baliano Grilli were insurers or bankers. The important thing for Zaccaria was to ensure that his ship and merchandise would reach their destination. In case of loss at sea, it was essential for him to avoid a disastrous bankruptcy that would have endangered his future business, and providing this avoidance was the primary task for Suppa and Grilli. These days, the virtual economy fulfils the same role, albeit on a much broader scale. Banks and insurance companies are not poles apart, since that they both meet the challenges thrown up by the real economy. Thus, any meticulous inventory of their institutional differences can be quite misleading. By seeing them through "virtual glasses", the careful economic observer will see through the rather superficial differences and focus on the issues that really matter.

Careful analysis shows that, in the main, insurance companies do indeed market options. Can they therefore remain competitive in the face of the formidable development of derivatives markets? Insurers could argue that the options that they sell to policyholders are highly complex. This complexity arises from the well-known phenomenon of *moral hazard*. Insurers fear negligent, or even fraudulent, behaviour on the part of policyholders. In addition, they also face difficulties in assessing the actual true risks of their policyholders. To use the jargon of the options market, insurance companies have a rather difficult task determining the exact *volatility* of the underlying asset they are insuring. In other words, it is not easy for insurers to calibrate precisely the risk category to which a given policyholder should be assigned. Insurers are intimately acquainted with this phenomenon, which is known as *anti-selection*. The smooth performance of contracts is jeopardized when insurers lack information on clients and this goes some way to explaining why insurers are obliged to structure insurance policies that may seem both extremely complex, and possibly unfair, to policyholders. Deductibles, bonuses, penalties and limits on covers are just some of the many safeguards which may be present to ensure the viability of insurance contracts. Baliano Grilli and Enrico Suppa faced similar obstacles when they agreed to cover Benedetto Zaccaria's risk. For example, there was no way of knowing whether Zaccaria would not be tempted to declare the loss of his goods even though they had reached their destination. Naturally, to counter this risk, Suppa and Grilli could have hired an assistant to travel with Zaccaria and monitor the precious cargo. Upon arrival in Bruges, the cargo could have be checked immediately by another assistant. While this is not a perfect solution, since it would have increased the costs of Grilli and Suppa, it would nevertheless have minimized the risk of fraud.

In the professional parlance of insurers, the *producer* is the underwriter who writes the insurance policy. However, the virtual economy shows that the true producer is the financier who has to prepare the relevant ingredients, i.e. the financial assets needed to guarantee successful completion of the insurance policy. The financial markets provide forums where companies can gather the financial inputs required in order to match their liabilities. This is where the very notion of asset-liability management pops into the picture. Thus, derivative instruments can be seen as useful tools which an insurance company can rely upon to meet the functions demanded by its client base.

The lesson is clear. Functions are always senior to institutions (see Merton, 1997) or, to put it more crudely, the client's needs are paramount. That said, the growing importance of virtual finance should not strike fear into the hearts of insurance companies. On the contrary, by shifting the focus of attention from institutions to functions, the virtual economy empowers market players (including visionary insurance companies) to use their imagination to improve their services. Far from disrupting the real economy, then, virtual finance improves its vitality. In conclusion, it should be clear that, for once at least, the big bad financial wolf is the good guy, and not the cruel and unpredictable tyrant that many observers fear.

Baliano Grilli and Enrico Suppa clearly knew a thing or two about seagoing dangers when they removed Benedetto Zaccaria's risks of pirates and storms nine centuries ago! Their task was undeniably difficult and it must be revisited and, indeed reinvented, time and again. However, at least one aspect can remain unchanged and that is their assertion that insurance underwriting and derivatives writing are, in practical terms, synonymous.

References

Favier, J., *De l'Or et des Épices, Naissance de l'Homme d'Affaires au Moyen-Age*, Flammarion, Paris (1987)

Wright, K.M., "The Structure Conduct and Regulation of the Life Insurance Industry", in R.W. Kopcke and R.E. Randall (Eds), *The Financial Condition and Regulation of Insurance Companies*, Federal Reserve Bank of Boston (1991)

Chapter 7

Conclusion and Future Challenges

Insurance pricing relates to the pricing of risks that are not, as yet, tradable. Indeed, after portfolio diversification *à la* Markowitz, insurance appears as the least costly technology available to get rid of unwanted risks. Residential real estate is a good example of such a situation: usually representing a significant part of the net worth of many households, it contains inherent concentrations of risk that cannot be easily diversified. For example, if one considers fire or burglary casualties, it is clearly impossible to mitigate these risks by having the kitchen in Omaha, the living room in New York City and the bedrooms in Los Angeles! In practice, the only way to cover these contingencies is through regular household insurance plans. To handle these risks, insurance companies need to rely upon the law of large numbers (i.e. the expected value principle) and their balance sheet (i.e. the standard deviation, or *"the expected value is not to be expected"*). This explains why, as we noted in the first chapter, actuaries tend to price risks on a "stand-alone" basis.

In contrast, capital market pricing relates to the pricing of risks that *are* tradable. Thus, investment banks are able to price these risks and take them on because they know how to hedge them efficiently. For example, hedging an interest rate swap to receive a floating rate in exchange for a fixed rate is "plain vanilla" business for investment banks. Hence, relative pricing, also called *no-arbitrage pricing*, has become the foundation for pricing financial derivatives. A derivative asset is priced with respect to its underlying asset and so option traders are able to quote prices because they can replicate their payoff by constructing a proper hedging portfolio. In other words, the key lies in the tracking (replicating) portfolio, the cashflows of which mimic that of the derivative asset to be priced. No-arbitrage means that the price of the derivative asset is equal to that of its tracking portfolio. Therefore, it stands to reason that, in the absence of a proper tracking portfolio, investment banks are unable to offer a proper risk menu.

Recently, talk of convergence between the insurance markets and the capital markets has become topical (if not the height of fashion!) within the financial world. Of course, in terms of pure function, an insurance policy can be classed as a put option, in that it delivers a protection against downside risk—that is to say, it guarantees a value to a contractually-specified asset. In reinsurance markets, excess-of-loss and stop-loss treaties also have option-like profiles. However, it is worth repeating that the actual asset underlying an insurance policy is rarely tradable. Moreover, its true inherent risk is not readily observable (anti-selection) and may change once insured (moral hazard). Nevertheless, insurance markets and capital markets are of a similar breed in that they share a similar risk-shifting function, even though they price and transfer different risks and, as we have noted, those risks are tradable for the capital markets and largely non-tradable for the insurance markets. In many real-life situations, though, risks are intermingled and actually contain both tradable and non-tradable elements. It is also a fact that the capital markets are engaged in a ceaseless quest to sweep away the limits of tradability and this is most notable in the area of securitization.

However, if the limits are truly to be swept away, the task that remains is quite enormous. Yale economist Robert J. Shiller aptly reminds us that there is actually a *lack* of financial markets! In the US, the equity market (that is, the market for claims on corporate dividends) accounts for a mere 3% of the national income.

So can the process of convergence be summarized in a nutshell? Well, ignoring regulatory differences for the moment, Figure 7-1 encapsulates the basic notions.

Convergence does, however, bring with it some significant difficulties, chief among them being accounting and regulatory problems. In June 1998, the US Financial Accounting Standards Board issued Statement no. 133, *Accounting for Derivative Instruments and Hedging Activities*. (Implementation of FAS133 is required as of 1 January 2001.) The background to this initiative is the strongly-held belief that the fair

> **INSURANCE = FINANCE WITHOUT A TRACKING PORTFOLIO, BUT WITH A BALANCE SHEET**
>
> **FINANCE = INSURANCE WITHOUT A BALANCE SHEET, BUT WITH A TRACKING PORTFOLIO**
>
> *These can be translated into:*
>
> **INSURANCE + FINANCE = IMPROVED RISK-SHARING OPPORTUNITIES AND THUS MUTUALLY-PROFITABLE BUSINESS OPPORTUNITIES**

Figure 7-1   A summary of the convergence process

valuation of any financial instrument carried by the balance sheet should be the rule, rather than the exception. Of course, this is relatively easy when the instrument is traded on a liquid market, but is far less so when the instrument is either not tradable at all, or features a complex structure comprising many sub-components. A typical example of this is an instrument that contains embedded derivatives. In such a case, a "bifurcation rule" prevails. The embedded derivatives are bifurcated (divided into two branches) from their host and are accounted for separately if their (economic) parameters are significantly different from that of the host. A good example of such a situation is that of life insurance policies that pay policyholders an above-market coupon in exchange for the shorting of a put option on a stock index. Policyholders receive a high coupon because the principal of their policies is exposed to a downfall in the stock market. FAS133 will henceforth require the isolation and valuation of the stock index put option.

However, the issues raised by FAS133 are somewhat complex and, in a way, they bring us back to both the first and fifth chapters of this book. We have seen that one of the major developments within the life insurance industry has been the growth of savings products—becoming the lion's share of the business. An ever-increasing number of annuity products contain embedded options, thus making them tantamount to highly-structured financial products. As we have noted, the advent of FAS133 will force actuaries to implement a fair valuation of the various components underlying these policies. However, despite the numerous professional task forces that have been set up, the fact remains that actuaries are not as yet familiar with this type of exercise. Indeed, as emphasized earlier, insurance has been thus far occupied with the taking of risks which are not tradable and, hence, not marked-to-market.

In point of fact, the problem for actuaries is far worse than it initially appears. Paragraph 51c of FAS133 requires the fair value exercise to be implemented at the policy inception date. This is a thorny task, requiring a rewind to plug in the parameters prevailing at the start date of the policy. Admittedly, insurance companies will benefit from a grand-fathering clause for policies issued prior to 1999, but this is only a mild relief. In any event, insurance companies will have develop proper financial and actuarial expertise to comply with FAS133. In a sense, though, such a regulatory move was to be expected. The boundaries between the insurance markets and the capital markets have become increasingly blurred for some time and, for regulatory, arbitrage and marketing reasons, insurance companies have been acquiring an increasing number of risks which are actually traded on financial markets. In fact, insurance companies are, in some cases, both more efficient and better placed than banks to carry risks or securities. An important difference between banks and insurance companies is that the former are bound by the stringent Basle regulatory (risk-based) capital criteria, whereas insurance companies, as we have noted, enjoy a less-strict regime. *Risk surgery*, the stripping and allocation of risks between banks' balance sheets and insurance companies' balance sheets, can thus be undertaken by a straightforward regulatory capital arbitrage. This arbitrage can last as long as insurance companies enjoy their preferential accounting and regulatory treatment.

In any case, and whatever one may think about the current and forthcoming regulatory initiatives, the trend is quite clear: insurance companies will have to shift their focus *from underwriting to derivatives*.

Appendix

The ALM Survival Toolkit
Fundamental issues to be addressed by the ALM manager

Section 1: Strategic considerations

Why equity in an insurance company or surplus in a pension fund?

- In a perfect world where insurance and pension pricing would be totally accurate (no actuarial risk):
  - insurance premium and pension contribution cash inflows match exactly claims cash outflows and pension payments;
  - and equity or surplus (in a defined benefit pension plan) is obviously redundant.

- Insurance pricing is however not accurate. . .
  - for instance, the law of large numbers is only an approximation;
  - longevity risk is currently a serious issue;
  - adverse selection may jeopardize the equilibrium of a portfolio of individual defined-contribution plans;
  - hence, a cushion is needed to absorb a variety of risks that are not fully captured by the insurance premium.

- This cushion has to be pre-committed in order to avoid ex-post moral hazard.

- Hence, pledging equity does make sense, even though it turns out to be the most costly source of funds.

1

Equity as a risk distribution mechanism

- Equity investors typically expect high average returns...
  - this is largely because equities have large amounts of undiversifiable risks;
  - they move strongly with the stock market and the stock market is volatile.

- Equity investors:
  - tend to prefer "pure plays"—that is, a pure high risk/high return investment;
  - would rather not have "the reward dilution" of co-mingled risk exposures, such as cat or interest rate risk exposures.

- In other words, equity investors expect a long-lived, complex risk (that they cannot easily duplicate).

- Equity risks are, therefore, not targeted to precise events over precise periods of time.

2

Equity as a risk distribution mechanism

- Insurance companies can maximize their value by taking risks that do not qualify as equity risks and letting them trade on separate markets, whether derivatives markets, reinsurance markets or debt markets.

- The statement above clearly begs the question of what type of risks do not qualify as equity risks, and this is precisely one of the tasks of modern Asset & Liability Management.

- Once this is done, the insurance company can use different tools to make its stock even more appealing ("disentangling" the signal from the unwanted noise) and can:
  - reshuffle its asset allocation;
  - use derivatives;
  - implement reinsurance programmes;
  - sell some lines of business;
  - and/or fine-tune its capital structure.

3

The life insurance company as a swap

- In a sense, an insurance company can be viewed as a swap:
  - for instance, a life insurance company typically receives fixed flows from its assets (coupons from its government bonds) and pays a combination of fixed and floating flows through its liabilities (minimum rate + bonus mechanism);
  - the same analogy can be drawn for a pension plan that swaps asset cashflows for pension liabilities cashflows.

- Hence, if nothing is done to prevent it, one can expect that the market capitalization of the insurance company will exhibit a fairly significant sensitivity to gyrations in the term structure of interest rates.

- Is this good, or bad, news for shareholders?

4

The example of life insurance contracts

- Issuing life insurance contracts is tantamount to borrowing money in a highly structured fashion.

- Indeed, policyholders are entitled to future cashflows which are governed by a number of contractual provisions that behave like options—such as guaranteed interest rates, surrender options, bonus, policy loan options, extension option, guaranteed annuity options, etc.

- These options may jeopardize the ability of the insurance company to generate a strong and sustainable embedded value, or the ability of the pension fund to accumulate a sizeable surplus.

- In other words, borrowing money through life insurance contracts or pension liabilities may turn out to be a costly exercise—even though the insurance company may enjoy the benefits of, say, a strong distribution franchise.

5

The example of life insurance contracts

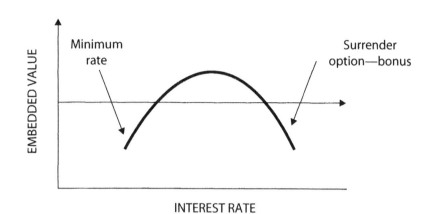

6

The example of life insurance contracts

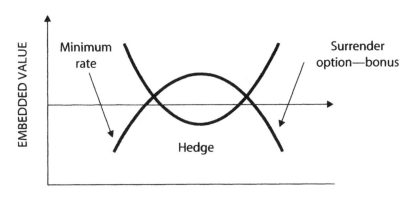

EMBEDDED VALUE

Minimum rate

Surrender option—bonus

Hedge

INTEREST RATE

7

The shareholders' pressure

* Shareholders are more and more demanding. . .
  - they want to invest in corporations that have superior knowledge and/or benefit from franchises that are not easily duplicated;
  - as such, they are increasingly willing to penalize corporations that do not remove unwanted risks from their balance sheets, especially when tools to do so do exist.

8

Section 2: ALM implementation

Need for rational asset & liability management

- The life insurance and pension industries and their competitive environment:
  - pressure of shareholders for higher returns;
  - pressure of competition among financial institutions for savings;
  - pressure of rating agencies for notations.

- Need for rational asset/liability management:
  - understanding the driving forces of value-added;
  - meeting profit return objectives, while managing risk and pressure of competition, rating agencies and regulators.

- Need to consider integrated solutions for life insurance companies:
  - investment policy and asset benchmarking;
  - hedging policy;
  - funding opportunities in the capital securities markets.

9

Need for rational asset & liability management

Capital Markets

· Financial conditions
· Investment universe
· Hedging instruments

Liabilities Structure

· New/existing portfolios
· Currency-denominated, unit-linked
· Embedded options
· Time horizon

Funding Structure

· Equity/debt structure
· Regulatory environment

Competitive Environment

· Underwriting/marketing policy
· Profit return objectives
· Rating agencies pressure

Risks

· Investment portfolio
· Financial risk exposure
· Event risk exposure
· Solvency margin requirements

Liabilities Fair Valuation
+
Risk Assessment

Asset Allocation
+
Profit Testing

10

From risk minimization to risk mitigation

- Risk minimization:
  - financial risk is undesirable and should be minimized;
  - financial risk should be isolated and monitored with the objective of keeping it as close to zero as possible.

- Risk mitigation:
  - a certain amount of financial risk may not be bad for a life insurance company;
  - deliberately taking on risk may allow the company better to meet its policyholders' needs and achieve its shareholders' long-range financial goals;
  - tendency to focus on the risk/return trade-offs.

11

How to define risk in an insurance company

- In order to measure and monitor risk, an insurance company has to evolve from static to dynamic measures of risk:
  - from a mean/variance approach;
  - to a mean/downside risk framework.

- Mean/variance analysis cannot capture the connection between assets and liabilities:
  - risk is measured by the dispersion of returns around their average value;
  - an insurance company is not a total return account;
  - a mean/variance model for asset returns cannot tie assets and liabilities together in a meaningful way;
  - variance is not suitable for truncated risk distributions.

- Downside risk is measured by the shortfall probability:
  - different liabilities give rise to different shortfall risks;
  - defined-benefit pension plans are characterized by significant shortfall risks;
  - under-performance and time-horizon are crucial parameters in an insurance company because of varying requirements of policyholders, regulators and shareholders;
  - these parameters give rise to the need for risk to be measured and controlled by the probability of under-performance/bankruptcy over a specified time-horizon.

12

Value-added in an insurance company

- The surplus market value is defined as the surplus book value, plus the sum of risk-adjusted discounted future profits (losses).

- Value-added is defined as:
  - the difference between the market value and the book value of initial surplus; or
  - the sum of risk-adjusted discounted future profits (losses).

- Value-added is a complex function of (among others):
  - actuarial characteristics of liabilities;
  - the asset portfolio and its rebalancing rules;
  - the overall management policy of the balance sheet;
  - financial market conditions.

13

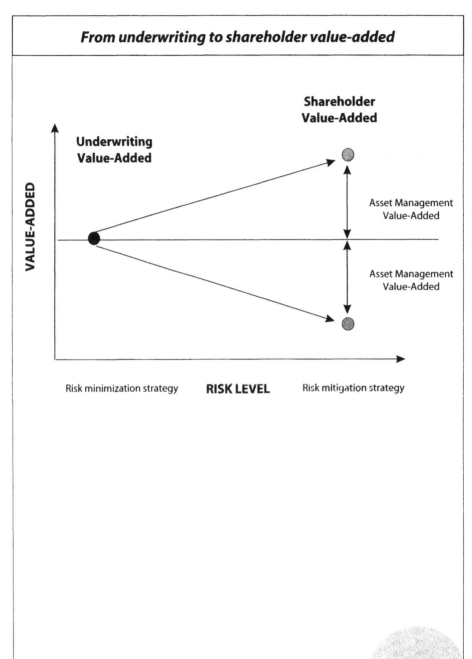

The example of interest rate risk exposure

- Surplus interest rate exposure is captured by the so called equity duration:
  - surplus of the insurance company is reduced (other things being equal) to its equivalent zero-coupon bond;
  - the maturity of this equivalent zero-coupon is the equity duration.

Balance sheet

	Market Value	Duration
Assets	A	D_A
Surplus	S	D_S
Liabilities	L	D_L

$$D_S = D_A + (D_A - D_L) * (L/S)$$

- Equity duration is a function of:
  - asset duration;
  - duration gap between assets and liabilities;
  - leverage of the insurance company.

15

Option-adjusted cost of capital

- The option-adjusted cost of capital is the discount rate required to value the shareholders' equity:
  - it incorporates the overall riskiness of surplus cashflows;
  - it is endogeneous to the insurance company.

Balance sheet

	Market Value	Discount Rate
Assets	A	R_A
Surplus	S	R_S
Liabilities	L	R_L

$$R_S = R_A + (R_A - R_L)*(L/S)$$

- The option-adjusted return on equity is the expected rate of return on the shareholders' initial investment.

- As soon as the return on equity is higher than the cost of capital, there is wealth creation for shareholders.

16

A comprehensive methodology

- Asset & Liability Management analysis must:
  - capture the various risks that the insurance company carries;
  - take into account the complex interaction between asset cashflows and liabilities cashflows;
  - consider the economic value of cashflows.

- A comprehensive methodology encompasses the whole asset and liability picture:
  - fair valuation of assets, liabilities and surplus;
  - asset portfolio benchmarking;
  - option-adjusted risk assessment;
  - profit testing.

17

A quantitative approach in three steps

Step #1   Underwriting Activity Audit
- ✔ Main objective — Audit the underwriting activity and define the underwriting results
- ✔ Output — Underwriting Value-Added (UVA)

    Immunizing asset duration
- ✔ Analytics — No financial risk

    Treasury bonds asset portfolio immunizing surplus

    Monte-Carlo simulations

Step #2   Investment Universe
- ✔ Main objective — Choice of specific asset portfolio benchmarks
- ✔ Output — Characteristics of benchmark

    Risk and return profiles
- ✔ Analytics — Investment constraints

    Choice of indices

    Portfolio model

Step #3   Asset Allocation & Profit Testing
- ✔ Main objective — Evaluate the value-added and the downside risk of each benchmark
- ✔ Output — Shareholder Value-Added (SVA)

    Probability of default
- ✔ Analytics — Financial and default risks

    Liabilities fair valuation

    Risk level assessment

    Monte-Carlo simulations

18

A stochastic simulation approach

Capital Market Assumptions

- Treasury yield curve
- Investment universe

Liabilities Modelling

- Actuarial data
- Balance sheet characteristics

Investment Simulations

- Quarterly rebalancing rules
- Buy/sell at market values

Cashflow Simulations

- Annual cashflows
- Accounting and regulatory constraints

Fair Valuation & Risk Assessment

- Risk adjusted and market value based analysis
- Asset allocation
- Profit testing

Simulations are performed under, say, 10,000 independent scenarios

19

Step #1: Underwriting activity audit

- An initial valuation is performed under 10,000 scenarios that are consistent with the current Treasury yield curve.

- The entire current term structure is then shifted (upwards and downwards) and a new valuation is performed.

Measuring market values and sensitivities

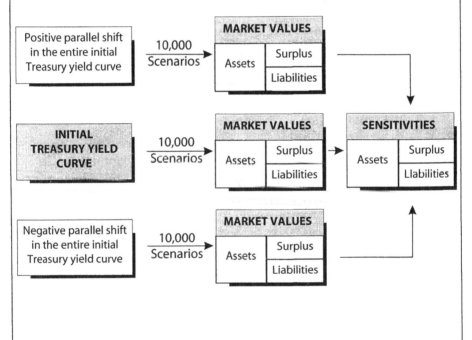

20

Step #2: Investment universe

- A good benchmark should include the following properties:
  - a well defined universe of investment;
  - investable securities;
  - daily performance, current characteristics and historical information available;
  - investment style clearly defined;
  - risk profile well defined.

- Investment portfolios are divided into two different funds:
  - a Treasury bond fund, the characteristics of which are determined during the underwriting activity audit;
  - a risky fund composed of different asset classes.

- The risky fund composition is determined according to:
  - authorized asset classes;
  - investment constraints;
  - a portfolio model framework.

21

Step #3: Asset allocation & profit testing

Input	✔ Initial Treasury yield curve
	✔ Financial market assumptions
	✔ Asset portfolio composition
	✔ Actuarial data
Time horizon	✔ Life of the fund (for instance, 25 years)
Stochastic generator	✔ Generate each quarter a new Treasury yield curve consistent with the interest rate model
	✔ Generate each quarter asset returns
Quarterly computations	✔ Treasury yield curve
	✔ Return on assets
	✔ Asset portfolio adjustments
Annual computations	✔ Annual return on assets (ROA)
	✔ Implied return on liabilities (ROL)
	✔ Discount rate
	✔ Cashflows (surplus, liabilities)
	✔ Solvency margin adjustment
Output	✔ Present value of future cashflows (surplus, liabilities) along to each scenario

22

Section 3:
Designing & implementing hedging

Hedging insurance liabilities

- When considering ways of reducing the exposure of identified liabilities, the insurance company may be interested in a solution that encompasses as many of the insurance company's business issues as possible:
  - provide economic protection;
  - structure the solution to be fully admissible under valuation regulations;
  - provide the best possible deal via transparency of pricing and efficiency of execution;
  - minimize counter-party risk;
  - achieve possible rating agency benefit;
  - release statutory capital to support solvency and for reinvestment in new business.

23

Risk transfer vs. cost

- In a perfect world, where insurance pricing would be totally accurate (no actuarial risk), insurance premium cash inflows match exactly claims cash outflows and equity is obviously redundant.

- However, insurance pricing is not accurate and pledging equity does make sense: a cushion is needed to absorb a variety of risks that are not fully captured by the insurance premium.

- However, equity turns out to be the most costly source of funds:
  - equity investors expect high average returns, because equities have large amounts of undiversifiable risks and move strongly with the (volatile) stock market;
  - equity investors tend to prefer "pure plays"—that is, a pure high risk/high return investment;
  - equity investors would rather not have "the reward dilution" of commingled risk exposures, such as cat or interest rate risk exposures;
  - equity investors expect a long-lived, complex risk (that they cannot easily duplicate).

- Equity risks are, therefore, not targeted to precise events over precise periods of time; one of the tasks of modern Asset & Liability Management is to identify what type of risks do not qualify as equity risks and have to be transferred.

- These risks can be separately, and more efficiently, carried:
  - markets do exist where these risks are traded and exchanged;
  - the most efficient way of hedging is given by "just-in-time" capital or contingent capital.

24

Optimizing regulatory, accounting and tax constraints

- Different forms of contingent capital can be used on derivatives markets, reinsurance markets or debt markets: the optimal choice will depend on regulatory, accounting and/or tax issues.

- Straight derivatives are the most widespread form of contingent capital.

- For an insurance company, derivatives may give rise to significant constraints:
  - Regulatory treatment. In many countries, insurance regulators do not consider derivatives as admitted assets.
  - Artificial volatility. If an obligation of marking them to market is made (although the underlying assets may be accounted on a book value rule), they can increase the P&L account volatility.
  - Insurance cycle & accounting risk. Although derivatives are performing tools providing economic risk transfer benefits, they cannot match perfectly the insurance cycle and hedge the accounting risk specific to the insurance industry.

- For an insurance company, reinsurance may provide several benefits:
  - traditional tool to hedge economic losses which appear progressively in the company accounts;
  - efficient way of performing a risk transfer from both an economic and accounting point of view;
  - potential reserving and solvency margin release;
  - standard regulatory, accounting and tax treatment.

25

A range of potential solutions

- Insurance companies may envisage a range of potential solutions to hedge their liabilities:

Asset-based solutions
1. Asset re-allocation (closer matching)
2. Straight derivatives
3. Structured notes

Liability-based solutions
4. Prudent reserving
5. Reinsurance
6. Subordinated debt
7. Securitization

26

Asset-based solutions

Solutions	Pros	Cons
1. Asset re-allocation (closer matching)	✔ "Simple"	✘ Limited availability of long dated assets ✘ Less efficient than derivatives
2. Straight derivatives	✔ Economic risk transfer ✔ Less structuring burden	✘ No accounting risk transfer ✘ Admissibility (?) ✘ Accounting rules/ Marked-to-market ✘ Administration/Back office
3. Structured notes	✔ Economic risk transfer ✔ Rating of the issuer ✔ Embedded derivatives	✘ No accounting risk transfer ✘ Cash drain ✘ Admissibility (?) ✘ Asset allocation

27

Liability-based solutions		
Solutions	**Pros**	**Cons**
4. Prudent reserving	✔ "Simple" ✔ Accounting risk transfer ✔ Tax deferral	✘ Limited risk transfer ✘ Costly balance sheet burden ✘ Solvency margin requirement
5. Reinsurance	✔ Accounting & economic risk transfer ✔ Full admissibility ✔ Potential reserving and solvency margin release ✔ Familiar tool	✘ Documentation ✘ Medium structuring burden
6. Subordinated debt	✔ Funding ✔ Rating	✘ Market capacity ✘ Increased disclosure ✘ Limited solvency margin benefit ✘ Structuring burden
7. Securitization	✔ Off balance-sheet funding	✘ Lengthy process ✘ Costly

28

Hedging insurance liabilities via reinsurance

- An efficient hedging strategy can be achieved via a reinsurance treaty:
  - reinsurance is a traditional tool for insurance companies to transfer risks;
  - reinsurance is particularly well designed to fit to (economic and accounting) specificities of the insurance industry;
  - reinsurance is a familiar technique, recognized by insurance companies and regulatory authorities.

- A step-by-step approach can be suggested to implement a reinsurance treaty:
  - assess the size and the characteristics of the cover;
  - choose the reinsurer;
  - execute solution according to the insurance company's efficiency and transparency guidelines.

29

Hedging insurance liabilities via reinsurance

- The reinsurance treaty covers the ceding insurer against the economic and statutory impacts of adverse fluctuations in long term interest rates and/or returns on assets
  - contractual provisions (minimum guaranteed rate, extension, surrender...)
  - application of specific provisions envisaged by the regulation (for example, reserving)
  - competition pressure (obligation to serve bonuses beyond what would be desirable from an actuarial point of view)

- Moreover the reinsurance treaty includes a specific mechanism of accounting smoothing intended to cover:
  - the more or less fast emergence of the losses
  - a possible aggravation of the losses noted initially

- The mode of reinsurance is a stop loss treaty

Principle

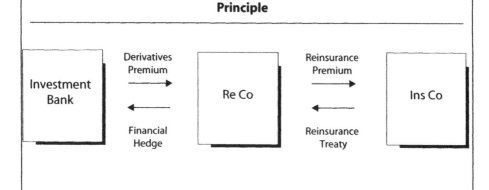

30

Hedging insurance liabilities via reinsurance

- The reinsurance premium has the following characteristics:
  - it may be single or periodic;
  - it may be reserved and deposited with the ceding insurer;
  - it may be pledged by the reinsurer with the ceding insurer according to local regulation.

Effective Date

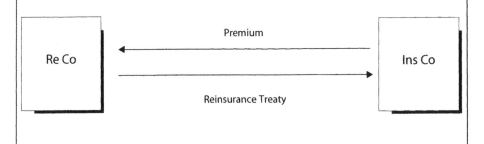

31

Hedging insurance liabilities via reinsurance

- On each payment date:
  - the reinsurer pays to the ceding insurer the accounting losses;
  - the remainder is reserved in a claims fund intended to mitigate the possible aggravation of the losses noted initially;
  - when the ceding insurer notes an aggravation of the losses, the reinsurer pays a complementary indemnity until exhaustion of the claims fund.

- The claims fund:
  - is not individualized per year of cover;
  - may be reserved with the ceding insurer;
  - may be pledged by the reinsurer with the ceding insurer under the conditions envisaged by the regulation.

Payment Date

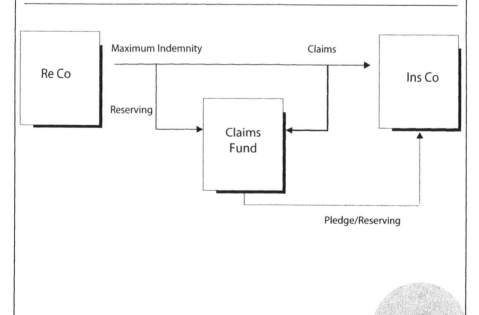

32

Hedging insurance liabilities via reinsurance

- If at maturity the claims fund is positive, it is credited entirely to the ceding insurer in the form of premium retrocession and/or no-claims bonus.

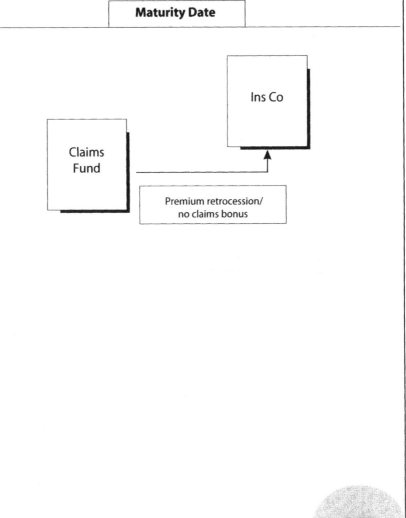

Maturity Date

Ins Co

Claims Fund

Premium retrocession/ no claims bonus

33

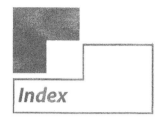

Index

Printed and bound by CPI Group (UK) Ltd, Croydon, CR0 4YY

23/04/2025

14660968-0004